College Connections™

for

CollegeFreshmen

Cheryl Gordon
Lynne Vagt

ISBN 978-0-578-06133-7

Printed in the United States of America.

For information, please e-mail info@greatchoicesonline.com.

Table of Contents

Introduction

Like the famed climbers of exhilarating mountain expeditions, college freshman find themselves ascending, not to a narrow peak, but to a new world—leaving high school behind, they move into the higher altitudes of college. Students who acquire the skills to move to higher camps and connect to fellow climbers will find the challenging college terrain inspires them to conquer new territory and explore new horizons.

Successfully navigating the early days of college hinges on the connections you make between the skills and experiences of the past and the challenges and opportunities of the future—gleaning understanding from lengthy lectures, using critical thinking skills in daily reading, managing time through extensive research projects, and making friends in close quarters.

College Connections™ is designed to be a practical support and helpful guide in your transition to college. Whether you work through this book independently, in a seminar or small group, or with a mentor or partner, *College Connections*™ will help you connect your past experiences to your present circumstances and your existing knowledge to the new expectations of college.

Each section in this book focuses on specific aspects of life and learning in college. You may choose to work front to back, back to front, or pick and choose the sections that interest you. Some sections may take you into new territory, while others may cover familiar terrain, serving as a not-so-subtle reminder to apply what you already know. Consider the structure and scope of your *College Connections*™ personal guidebook:

- The Differences Between High School and College
- Your Brain and Learning
- Managing Your Time
- Listening and Note-taking
- Reading and Retaining
- Writing and Research
- Testing and Problem Solving
- Campus Life

At the beginning of each section, a case study introduces you to a story about other students and the college experiences that demonstrate their need for the particular skills or understandings discussed in that section. At the end of each case study, you will find questions that will help connect these real world stories to your personal experiences. Those experiences shape your unique personal story, serving as the foundation for your path to success. Regardless of the strength of this foundation, you will find that as you enter college, there is much you can do now to become better equipped for success throughout college. The activities and reflections that follow each case study will support you in that process, taking you beyond simply reading information and guiding you into using tools and applying skills for success throughout your college experience.

It has been said that expectations drive outcomes—that the results of any endeavor are shaped by what you expect those results to be. That bit of common wisdom is worth writing in your travel notes. Your expectations of yourself during college will drive the outcome of your college experience. *College Connections*™ is packed with tools to support you on your journey. Whether you work through this guide with others or independently, keep it close at hand as a ready reference tool to help you navigate your successful college journey.

You have brains in
your head,
you have feet in
your shoes,
You can steer yourself
in any direction you
choose.
You're on your own
and you know what
you know,
you are the guy who'll
decide where to go.

Dr. Seuss

differencesbetweenhigh

school&collegedifference

A Case Study: 1.1 Learning at the College Level

Joe and Kimi were discussing the upcoming psychology exam. Frustrated by the task of remembering and describing the many names and theories they were responsible for knowing, Kimi closed her book, turned off her laptop, and handed Joe's notes back to him. "I give up," she said. "This is impossible—I am not a psychology major, why do I have to learn all these names and theories? They have nothing to do with me."

Joe nodded sympathetically, but quickly responded! "Think about it, Kimi! If you are studying countless facts and principles that do not seem to be even remotely related to what you want to do, you are not going to remember them, let alone understand them. You really have to look at all of those facts and principles as pieces of a puzzle that fit together and make up a much bigger picture!"

"Easy for you to say. Everything made sense when Professor Lang lectured and when I read the text and most of the supplemental readings, but now it is all just a confusing pile of facts, names, and theories!" Kimi retorted.

"Okay, I get that; but getting the big picture takes time. Where are your class notes, reading notes, and daily summaries? We can start to sort this out by going back to the beginning," Joe replied encouragingly. "What study methods work best for you?"

Kimi's groan and dejected look told her story better than words. In the chaos of residence hall living and adapting to college life, note-taking and daily studying had been placed—not so neatly—on the back burner. And Kimi's study methods were becoming like the rusty clippers she left out in the yard last winter—they were losing their edge.

Joe took the lead and suggested that Kimi meet him at the library after dinner, so that they could lay out a few of the main ideas from each lecture, look over Kimi's notes and handouts, and begin to organize an approach to the coming exam. Kimi was skeptical, but appreciated Joe's offer. Joe encouraged her, saying that with focus and direction, she could make a lot of headway in a short time.

Joe assured Kimi that helping her study was going to give him a great review of his notes and materials. Kimi decided that she had nothing to lose and if she could at least pass the first exam, she would be set to keep up for the rest of the semester.

Think it Over, Write it Out.

With the pace and distractions of their first six weeks of college, Joe and Kimi unequivocally agreed, this isn't high school anymore! What clues do you see in their story that indicate they are not in high school?

Before they arrived on campus, Joe and Kimi certainly knew that college and high school would be different. What do you think they were thinking when they said, "This isn't high school anymore?"

Could they have prepared for the differences between high school and college? What can they do now that they are six weeks into the semester to make the rest of this term a little smoother?

Who gained the most in the study plan, Joe or Kimi? What difficulties will Kimi face in catching up?

How well does Kimi expect to do on her exam? How well do you think she can do? What suggestions do you have for Joe and Kimi?

Out With the Old – In With the New

During college orientation, leaders briefed you on many issues relevant to your new life: residence hall rules, lost key procedures, registration and drop deadlines, cafeteria hours, campus maps, cell phone reception, email passwords, medical facilities, parking permits, parking fines, parking restrictions, and the list goes on and on and on. Joe and Kimi are right—college isn't high school. To get a closer look at what college is, let's stop, rewind, and start again by taking a stab at the question: What makes college so different from high school?

One seasoned college student answered that question quickly—personal freedom—there's no one to tell you what you must do! Most college students agree with that conclusion. The good news is—in college you have a lot of personal freedom and the bad news is—in college you have a lot of personal freedom! Well, that isn't really bad news, but with personal freedom comes personal responsibility and that can be daunting!

So let's begin to address the heart of this difference between high school and college. A brief discussion and analysis of personal freedom as it is limited or expressed in academic life during high school and college will go right to the heart of those differences. According to the transitions website at Southern Methodist University, major differences include classes, exams, grades, and professors.

Personal Freedom

Look at personal freedom as a continuum. As a growing child, your parents and teachers taught you responsibility and independence. You went from crawling to walking to running. Soon you were reading and writing, choosing friends, learning to drive, acquiring a license, and assuming growing responsibility for managing your time and money. Until age 18, your independence was guarded by rules and responsibilities. Even the law said you were a minor—not a major!

As the high school years end, the college years take up that continuum of personal responsibility and freedom. As a college student, you assume many of the daily responsibilities others may have previously performed for you or shared with you—laundry, meals, car maintenance, etc. You have likely reached the milestone of age 18, and with that milestone comes the freedom of greater privilege and the burden of greater accountability for your choices.

Compare the personal responsibility of a college freshman to that of a high school student. Write your thoughts and observations in the reflection below. As you look at each topic listed, ask these questions:

- What is different in this area?
- Who was responsible last year?
- Who is responsible this year?

Reflection 1.2: High School and College

Topic	High School	College
Control of your time		
Signature/ permissions required		
Rules and reminders		
Establishing priorities		
Your moral and ethical decisions		

Step back and take a look at what you wrote and consider what another student said. Ryan, a college freshman home for the winter break, simply stated, "When you go to college, it's all on you. You are the one to decide if you go to class, study, or play ultimate Frisbee, – but I say, go to class, it helps!"

After completing the reflection, it's pretty easy to see the truth in Ryan's statement, "It's all on you." That statement may cause some students to panic and others to cheer. Either way, this is the reality of your college years, and it permeates every aspect of your college world: classes, testing, grades, and instructors and professors.

It is safe to say that the changing expression of personal freedom and personal responsibility is central to the differences you experience as you leave high school and enter college. For most students, the high school expressions of personal freedom and personal responsibility were always influenced by the guiding principle that: "You will usually be told what to do and corrected if your behavior is out of line."[1]

Look back at Reflection 1.2, consider Ryan's statement on page 7, and reflect on the guiding principle for high school life suggested above. In a brief statement, describes the relationship between personal freedom and responsibility as expressed in your college life.

Reflection 1.3: Personal Freedom and Responsibility

In the next few pages, you will compare the freedoms and responsibilities you experienced during high school with those you will experience or have experienced during college. Your comparison will include your college classes, studying, testing, grades, and with your college instructors and professors.

Classes

By now you realize that your college classes are structured to reflect the independent spirit of college life. Gone are the days of fighting the crowded high school hallways, being directed by a rigid bell schedule, and elbowing your way to the locker bays! While college provides many crowded and sold out sporting events, class schedules vary widely. You may have early morning and afternoon classes, while your friend may be enrolled primarily in evening classes. Take a few minutes, once again, to compare the attributes of your classes and studies now to where you were a year ago.

---

1   "How is College Difference that High School?"*Southern Methodist University*, 24 June 2009 <http://smu.edu/alec/transition.asp>.

Write your reflections in the form below. Again, as you think about each topic, ask these questions:

- What is different in this area?
- Who was responsible last year?
- Who is responsible this year?

Reflection 1.4: High School and College Classes

Topic	High School	College
Class schedules		
Time in class		
Amount of study time required for success		
Frequency of assignments and exams		
Expectations for learning from reading assignments*		
Attendance requirements		
Class size		
Cost of textbooks		

* In other words, does the teacher or professor explain what you need to learn from your assigned readings or expect that you have already read and learned what is needed?

When you completed the "high school" part of the reflection, did you notice how much of your high school learning occurred within the classroom? High school policies require that you attend class regularly and give you multiple opportunities to demonstrate and develop your understanding of materials through projects, assignments, and exams. In so doing, you developed important learning skills and tools.

Consider the "college" column of your class reflection closely. Ask yourself how the guiding principle you wrote for college life (in the last section) is experienced in the way college classes are structured and learning is expressed inside and outside of those classes. If high school classes operate from the perspective that high school's external structure will help ensure that you learn what is required, how would you describe the role and structure of college classes in your approach to learning now? Write your thoughts below.

Reflection 1.5: College Classes

As you transfer and apply your understanding of freedom and responsibility to the many aspects of academic life in college, you will begin to define an approach to learning that fits you, your experiences, your goals, and your new world. This approach will guide you as you make daily choices that impact your learning success. With that in mind, move on and consider the implications these same principles have on your testing experiences.

Testing

Toni called home after her first college exam, frustrated, disappointed, and a little angry. "I studied harder for that exam than I did for any exam during all my years of high school." This disgruntled former high school valedictorian student received the first "C" of her academic career. Shocked, she begged her parents to let her come home: Toni didn't feel ready for college.

At this point, you may or may not have taken your first college exam. Throughout high school, you probably found that the first test given in each of your fall classes helped you to prepare for the tests to come; that first exam often came during the first two weeks of a single term or a full year class. In contrast, Toni's first ever college exam came only two weeks before her midterms, catching her completely off guard. Toni found herself out-of-touch with her professor's expectations.

You may notice that college exams are usually given less frequently than high school exams and therefore each college exam counts heavily in your overall grade. Complete this next reflection to identify the differing role of exams during high school and college. If you have not had your first college exam, discuss exam policies with upper class students, professors, advisors, and others, and review exams listed in your class syllabi before you complete Reflection 1.6.

Reflection 1.6: High School and College Tests

Topic	High School	College
Frequency of testing in each class		
Length of exams		
Weight of each exam in grading equation		
Testing as a learning experience		
Testing as an assessment of mastery		
In-class reviews for exams		
Scheduling of exams related to campus events		
Make up exams		

Whether you have already sweated through your first college exams or only heard tales of filling a twenty-page blue or green book in a three-and a-half-hour session, it is crucial to realize that testing at the college level may be drastically different than at the high school level. For example, testing dates are usually printed in the course syllabus and seldom change. You are responsible for all material presented and assigned. Make-up exams are seldom allowed.

Consider how the differences you have explored thus far are reflected in the way testing is handled in college. How do those differences impact the way you think, study, and prepare for exams? Write your thoughts below.

Reflection 1.7: College Exams

Grades

On the surface, independence and responsibility seem a little removed from grades. But take a closer look at grading in college: Colleges do not report five week grades, award bonus points for on-time work, and may not offer uniform grading scales. The standard for passing a course within your major may differ from that of a general education course or courses in another major. Grades are a reflection of your ability to meet the objectives of each course as outlined in the syllabus. Professors assess your ability to apply learning through your performance in a lab, on an exam, or in research and writing, and they award points according to the scale published in the course syllabus, which may be unique to the professor, the discipline, or university. Does this sound like your high school grade report? Probably not!

As you continue to consider the differences between high school and college, think about and compare grading experiences in high school and college. Take a minute and respond to the topics in the following reflection. As you complete the table, think about these questions:

- What is different in this area?
- Who was responsible last year?
- Who is responsible this year?

Reflection 1.8: High School and College Grades

Topic	High School	College
Frequency of graded assignments		
Extra credit opportunities		
Reminders of work due or exam dates		
Late work policies		
Weighting of each assignment in course grade		
Help available if you fall behind		

As you completed your grades reflection, did you find that many high school class activities and much of your interaction with teachers revolved around the topic of grades? While grades indicate a student's mastery of course expectations, high school grades often serve as an institutional signal that a student is struggling or failing. And while class attendance in high school is required, or compulsory, class attendance in college is usually optional. You don't have to go to college, and once you are there, you don't have to go to class. Based on those facts, colleges assume that students want to be there, want to succeed, and know how to learn. They expect students to be vested in learning and understanding the skills, concepts, and information necessary for success in broader fields of study. With that expectation comes the expectation that students will attend class without being told.

Looking at your reflection and the previous paragraph, how would you describe the role you expect grades to play in your college life?

Reflection 1.9 College Grades

Your Professors

Any discussion of classes, testing, and grades takes you back to the author of all three: the professor or instructor. Compared with the familiar teachers of your former high school, the faculty of the typical four-year college or university may be quite intimidating: large classes, formal lectures, impressive credentials, and specific office hours. But like any new community, given a little time and common experiences, you will develop a relationship with several of the esteemed faculty. The last few pages and the first few weeks of college make it clear that college professors and high school teachers have different expectations, styles, and goals for their students.

Go back over the comparisons you made in the last three reflections and write a paragraph or two about your professors' expectations of you, your coursework, and performance. Consider the professors' attitudes and expectations toward classes, testing, and grades and what those expectations will require of you as an independent and responsible college student.

Reflection 1.10: College Professors

Understanding Leads to Success

Yes, college and high school are different in many ways. When you understand those differences, you will begin using your study skills more effectively, choosing your learning tools more appropriately, and managing your time more efficiently, thus making the most of your college years. While the many experiences you had during high school helped equip and prepare you for the rigors and expectations of college, the real demands of college will now stretch you, compelling you to grow further. This workbook will review and reveal college level study tools and skills, help you tailor their use to your study goals, and integrate them into a formula that leads to college success.

Welcome to College Life 101!

Let's get started by taking a look inside your brain. How is your brain working these days? Everyone's brain is unique; with about one hundred billion neurons, this amazing computer successfully controls and processes information 24/7 without you even realizing it. Processing sensory input, forming and interpreting language, feeling and expressing emotion, storing and accessing memory, directing movement, and regulating many body processes are just some of the many functions your brain performs.

Why all this attention on the brain? Because during the college years, you will be more actively involved in acquiring, understanding, and applying new knowledge and skills than perhaps at any other time in your adult life. Better than your bright shiny new laptop, this bundle of neurons known as your brain will house your new knowledge and develop the increased intellectual skills that knowledge requires. Just as it helps to know your computer software, it really helps to know and understand your brain – how your mind works, what helps it work better, and what might cause it to "bog down, freeze, or crash." Taking time to understand and be good to your brain will help you do better in school, work, relationships, and life!

Think about it - How can you be good to your brain? The brain is a body organ that needs rest, nutrients, and exercise just like any other organ. How will you take care of yours as you move through the college years? Will you stress it with too many commitments? Will you deprive it of rest by staying up all night partying or studying? Will you starve if you eat a steady diet of junk food?

Live Well, Learn Well

When applied to healthy habits, living well can hold the key to academic success for college students. In recent years, studies have underscored the relationship between nutrition, exercise, and learning. The brain, as a body organ within the nervous system, responds to the same physiology that affects all organs; therefore, the building blocks of good health—sleep, nutrition, and exercise—are critical to good brain health.   Take a moment to consider how your decisions in these areas impact your overall brain health and specific cognitive performance.

Sleep

"Sleep on it" is more than a colloquialism. Brain researchers tested two groups of subjects, presenting them with math problems that they were to solve. The subjects were then given a twelve-hour break, during which one group slept for eight hours, while the other group did not sleep at all. Only 20% of those who did not sleep uncovered a shortcut and showed improvement in their ability to solve the assigned math problems. By contrast, 60%, or three times as many students who had eight hours of sleep discovered the shortcut. [2] Similar results are demonstrated in study after study, indicating that regular and adequate sleep is a critical to healthy brain functioning and learning.

2   Medina, John. *Brain Rules.* In *Sleep,* 161. Seattle: Pear Press, 2008. http://www.brainrules.net

Exercise

Healthy brains need good blood flow and oxygen, and exercise is a vital means of increasing both in your brain. As you step into the independence of college, making room for regular exercise is an important part of your academic success plan.   Research again backs the importance of exercise in healthy brain function and demonstrates that exercise is positively related to improved academic performance. By adding exercise to your daily routine, you facilitate your success now and build habits for success throughout your life.

Nutrition

"You are what you eat" is hardly a scientific finding, but it reflects the findings of countless studies that affirm the brain's need for adequate and appropriate food and water. If you already know that the body is largely water, it will not surprise you to learn that the brain is 80% water. But did you know that even mild dehydration was found to impede learning? Make it a point to drink plenty of liquids, particularly water.[3]

While you sleep, your blood glucose level falls, leaving your brain hungry for fuel. Eating a breakfast that includes protein will replenish your glucose stores and therefore, is a staple on the list of good eating habits. Throughout the day, your good food choices continue to supply energy and provide the many essential nutrients that promote a positive attitude, a good memory, and a strong ability to concentrate. Good meal choices, frequent healthy snacks, and a multivitamin will help to ensure that your body and your brain have the essential nutrients, including trace vitamins and minerals, that you need for optimum performance.

You will spend several years of your life and dedicate a significant amount of money to your college education. Others will define required standards of performance for your academic and perhaps, your athletic endeavors. Higher order thinking and effective short and long term memory will prove critical to your ability to learn and apply new concepts and skills in your studies and your activities—and while your diet, exercise, and sleeping habits will greatly influence your success in these areas, only you can control

---

3   Nut Shell Notes: Brain-based Learning 3—Nutrition for Scholarly Performance. Volume IX Number 1. Retrieved from http://www.isu.edu/ctl/nutshells/old_nutshells/9_1.htm

these critical personal decisions.   Do yourself a favor, get the most out of your studies by taking good care of your health and your BRAIN.

Brain Rules and You

Dr. John Medina, the director of the Brain Center for Applied Learning Research at Seattle Pacific University, lists twelve brain rules in his best selling book *Brain Rules*.[4] Read his list of rules below and identify those rules that you can apply to promote a healthy brain. Write those rules in the box provided.

1. Exercise promotes brain power.
2. The human brain evolved, too.
3. Every brain is wired differently.
4. We don't pay attention to boring things.
5. Repeat to remember.
6. Remember to repeat.
7. Sleep well, think well.
8. Stressed brains don't learn the same way.
9. Stimulate more of the senses.
10. Vision trumps all other senses.
11. Male and female brains are different.
12. We are powerful and natural explorers.

Reflection 2.1: Brain Rules

Rules that promote a healthy brain:

In addition to taking care of the physical brain, understanding ways to help your brain learn and retain information may help you improve your academic performance.

List some of the brain rules that suggest ways that your brain learns.

4   Medina, John. *Brain Rules*. Seattle: Pear Press, 2008. http://www.brainrules.net

Inspired by Dr. Medina's list of brain rules, describe some of the actions or habits you could adopt or continue in the year ahead to optimize your learning. For instance, if you sleep well already, write "sleep well" in the first column and check the "Will Continue " column. If you don't sleep well, skip column two and complete the sentence in column three describing how you can adopt this habit.

Reflection 2.2: Optimize Your Learning

Habits List	Will Continue	These are the changes I would have to make...

Researchers have long studied how the brain works and how learning occurs. In recent years, much attention has been paid to the concept of learning styles. While many theories exist to explain how learning occurs within the brain, one of the most practical applications of these theories is in the approach students take as they pursue their studies.

Simply explained, learning occurs when you take in information through the senses and then reflect and repeat what you have learned. That reflection and repetition occurs by thinking it over, discussing it, hearing related information, and writing it out. Learning continues when you analyze, evaluate, and then synthesize your new knowledge with previous knowledge and concepts and with principles from other disciplines. In other words, learning is not as simple as remembering new facts or identifying simple answers to problems. Learning requires that you understand and express new information in a variety of ways, transferring knowledge between topics, tasks, and skills.

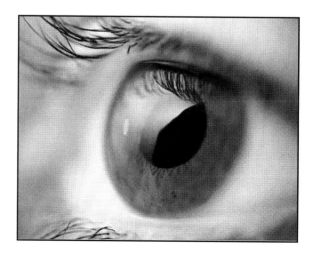

Students who learn well do not always learn in the same ways. Consider the ways two different students learn.

Case Study 2.3: Learning Preferences Expressed

Ruben and Hana met in their second semester physics class. They both loved the sciences, worked together in labs, and often studied together for their major exams. By the end of their third semester of college, they were veteran study partners. Ruben kept meticulous notes, and Hana took flash card creation to new heights.

Ruben knew before entering college that he learned better when he found or created visual cues that reinforced concepts or information. When he heard a professor lecture, he remembered it much better if he could see what he was learning. During high school, he developed a pretty thorough system for note taking and then faithfully reviewed those notes weekly and, sometimes, daily. He would use diagrams, colored ink, and symbols to emphasize key points and concepts within his notes. Following the Cornell Note-taking System, Ruben's kept highly effective and thorough notes. He believed that the key to his high AP scores was his consistent use of this excellent study tool.

Although Hana had always been a good student, she had not identified any specific learning style or preference before entering college. But after studying with Ruben and thinking about how she used her flashcards to prepare for exams, she decided that she must be very responsive to auditory cues. Hana's use of flash cards was just as disciplined as Ruben's use of good class notes. After each class and during each reading, Hana wrote flash cards for key terms, basic concepts, names, dates, principles, and any other information that she thought was pertinent to understanding the material she was learning. She then made time to review regularly, reading both sides of her cards, mixing their order, and sorting cards into various groups as she read them aloud.

Think it Over

How did Ruben adapt his note taking to incorporate his preference for visual cues? How did Hana incorporate her auditory preferences in her creation and use of flash cards? Can you think of other options these students might have used to meet their sensory learning preferences?

Why did Ruben and Hana learn more effectively studying together than studying alone? Have you had a similar experience when studying with someone using a different assortment of study skills or strategies?

Your Senses - Natural Learning Tools

Like Ruben and Hana, you may observe students who improve their retention of facts and understanding of concepts using visual cues (e.g., seeing and visualizing a graph) and others who enhance learning through audio cues (e.g., audibly repeating, hearing, and memorizing a list). Learning theories, which were developed over the last forty years, might identify these students as either visual learners or auditory learners.

Another category of learners often cited is that of kinesthetic/tactile learners—those who learn best by doing. These three learning styles or preferences comprise the VAK (visual, auditory, and kinesthetic) theory of learning. In 1987, Neil Flemming adapted the VAK theory by adding another type of learner to the mix: reading/writing learners (those who learn best through the written word—reading or writing). He named his theory VARK, an acronym for the fours types of learners—visual, auditory, reading/writing, and kinesthetic.

Whether or not you consider yourself to be a particular type of learner, it is important to note that all learning preferences offer valid paths to improved learning. While you may use study tools associated with one or two learning styles, over a lifetime of learning you will combine methods and tools associated with all of the styles. Understanding how your brain works and how you learn will help you make the most of your study time.

NOTE: Many theories exist to explain the complexities of how people learn. From the three VAK learning styles to the more complex theory of eight multiple intelligences (verbal linguistic, logical-mathematical, musical, spatial, bodily kinesthetic, interpersonal, intrapersonal, naturalist)[5], all learning theories stress the value of understanding how the

5   Gardener, Howard, Ph.D. "Intelligences in Seven Steps." *New Horizons for Learning* (1991): June 24, 2009 <http://www.newhorizons.org/future/Creating_the_Future/crfut_gardner.htmlv>.

individual learns and then applying that understanding to improved learning strategies or skills. Many inventories, explanations, and study coaches are available to assist you in better understanding your learning style, learning preferences, or multiple intelligences. These resources can be located through reputable education counselors or through college or university learning centers.

Ready, Set, Learn!

On a very practical, simple level, what do educational psychologists and other researchers say about learning?

- You must use your senses to acquire knowledge and experience: hear, see, taste, smell, touch, and movement.

- The more senses you engage in the learning process, the more you learn.

- Mental processing and repeated handling of information through the senses increases your retention of information.

- Higher order cognitive behaviors (analysis, synthesis, evaluation) increase your application and transference of learning. (You can apply what you have learned to new situations in creative ways.)

Answer the questions in the following reflection to examine what implications these four statements have for learning during your college years.

Reflection 2.4: Getting on Board to Learn

As you reflect on your learning experiences, consider the roles of a) sensory input, b) repetition, c) mental processing, and d) higher order thinking in your learning experiences.

1. Describe a time when you learned something new, very thoroughly and successfully.

2. Describe a time you struggled to learn something new and felt less than successful:

3. Comparing your two experiences, what made the difference between learning well and struggling?

4. What senses do you currently or expect to use when studying for your college classes?

5. In what specific ways can you use more of your senses more often as you prepare for your classes?

6. What strategies do you use to memorize facts? How do repetition and mnemonic devices (e.g., anonyms, silly sentences) aid your recall?

7. Explain a time this year or last year when you found yourself successfully analyzing, synthesizing, and evaluating ideas, processes, and materials that were taught in a class.

8. Who is responsible for your learning? Describe why.

9. If you need any help with a class, list three resources (i.e., people, programs) or three strategies that might help you (e.g., flash card reviews, group study sessions).

As you completed the reflection, did you find that you have employed specific learning strategies to understand challenging materials? Did you think about ways you learn that may be different from ways your friends learn? Did you think about teachers who made learning exciting?

Think of a time when you learned something exciting. Being interested in a topic increases your ability to remember and understand what you learn. The more you are interested, the more you think about new information and concepts, and the more you will strengthen the understandings and connections you make between the new material and past or present understanding and experiences.

Explain the implication of the following quote by G. K. Chesterton and describe ways that you can increase your interest in the topics and subjects you are studying.
"There are no uninteresting subjects, only uninterested people."

....
....
....
....

Investing in Your Future

Understanding how learning takes place, and how you as an individual learn—with your own experiences, preferences, struggles, and successes—will help you identify ways to improve your learning. Given the complexity and quantity of learning that must take place over the next four years, improved learning means less stress, more time, and a better value for the dollars you are investing in your education.

Time is what prevents everything from happening at once.

John Archibald Wheeler

Case Study 3.1: Time Management Options

Luis and Andrew are roommates in a freshman residence hall. They chatted online a couple of times over the summer and met for the first time when they arrived on campus. They were surprised to find they had a lot in common: both were majoring in business, both graduated in the top 20% of their high school classes, and both enjoyed soccer and swimming.

Luis found the first three weeks of college to be a rewarding challenge: getting to classes, preparing his readings, completing assigned labs, grabbing lunch with new friends, attending a couple student and community performances, playing intramural soccer, meeting with a professor or T.A., and hitting the library regularly. Although he was juggling more tasks and opportunities than ever before, Luis felt that in only a few short weeks, he had learned more than he ever thought was possible.

Andrew emerged from those same three weeks exhausted and frustrated. From the moment orientation ended, he felt like he was running to catch up. Most of his first week was spent finding where his classes met. Falling behind in checking his e-mail, Andrew frequently missed deadlines: he overlooked three important messages from T.A.s and professors and was assessed a fine when he missed a construction notice about freshman parking restrictions. With a different class schedule everyday, Andrew literally didn't know whether he was coming or going. He woke up on his fourth Saturday morning on campus feeling weary and wondering how he was going to make it through the semester. Stress was quickly overwhelming the previously energetic Andrew.

Andrew and Luis would describe the activities, demands, and opportunities of the initial weeks of college differently. Both were strong students in high school, and since arriving on campus, they had very common experiences—the same classes, the same residence hall, the same orientation, and the same support services. Both arrived excited to be attending their first choice school and to begin college life; however, you can see that before the first month was over, Luis found the environment invigorating, while Andrew found it draining.

Andrew's parents suggested that he stop in and talk to his R. A. (Resident Assistant) about his frustrations. Surprisingly, as Andrew described his situation, his R.A. began nodding his head saying, "I had the same problem my freshman year." He then walked Andrew to the Students Services Office where Andrew met with a student counselor. Two weeks later, when his R.A. came by to see how he was doing, Andrew told him that Student Services helped him set up a realistic weekly schedule that "saved his life."

Think it Over, Write it Out.

How does time impact Luis's daily living? How does time impact Andrew's daily living? How is each experiencing personal freedom and personal responsibility?

When Andrew was frustrated, he took some time and did several things to try and solve his problem. What steps did Andrew take to relieve his frustration? Can you think of other steps he might have taken? In what ways would it be hard or easy for you to do what Andrew did?

What's the magic in a schedule? Both Andrew and Luis had the same classes, similar abilities and interests, and similar high school success. Why did Luis adapt to college so easily? Did a written schedule help Andrew? Explain.

Implications

Entering college places students in the middle of a new and dynamic environment. As Luis and Andrew's experiences demonstrate, your transition to this new environment will be affected by several issues:

- Previous experiences
- Personal history
- Priorities
- Planning
- Forecasting
- Decision making
- Commitment

You will recall that the most significant difference between college and high school is that college offers a much higher level of independence and demands a much higher level of personal responsibility. Your success in meeting those demands will be determined in great measure by your ability to plan and utilize the skills necessary to implement your own schedule. As Luis and Andrew demonstrated, scheduling can make or break your early college experience.

Think about your schedule. How does time planning impact your daily living? Are you in control of your time and your activities? Would you like to make better use of your time?

As you begin your college career, you will soon find that no two days look alike. One day may be filled with morning classes, one with afternoon and evening classes, and one day may be completely open—no classes scheduled. How do you fill those empty spaces? Do you decide what you will do, or do you simply "hang out" and "go with the flow?" Think through the effectiveness of your time management system as you complete the following reflection.

Reflection 3.2: How is that working for you?

Method of planning my time now:
- ☐ Paper calendar
- ☐ Electronic
- ☐ Memory
- ☐ Other (explain) _____

I check my schedule this often:
- ☐ Multiple times daily
- ☐ Once a day
- ☐ Once every two or three days
- ☐ Once a week or less
- ☐ Never

Check one sentence in each group and make comments as needed:
- ☐ I am usually late to classes.
- ☐ I am usually on time to class.

Comment:_____

_____

- ☐ I never forget appointments, assignments or deadlines.
- ☐ I sometimes forget appointments, assignments or deadlines.
- ☐ I often forget appointments, assignments or deadlines.

Comment:_____

_____

- ☐ I usually complete each day with sense of accomplishment.
- ☐ I often complete each day frustrated and stressed because I did not accomplish what I wanted or needed.

Comment:_____

_____

- ☐ I feel confident about my priorities and how I am managing them.
- ☐ I feel uncertain of my priorities and how I am managing them.

Comment:_____

_____

- ☐ How I spend my time is not compatible with my direction and goals.
- ☐ How I spend my time is compatible with my goals.

Comment:_____

_____

- ☐ I usually get enough sleep, good nutrition, and adequate exercise.
- ☐ I usually do not get enough sleep, good nutrition, and adequate exercise.

Comment:_____

_____

As you reflect upon your answers to the previous questions, consider whether you are satisfied with how you are using your time. Circle any statement that indicates an area with room for improvement. Later in this section, you will select a time management tool or strategy to help you use your time more effectively.

More than a Routine

While your schedule may be different every day of the week, it is the unscheduled activities—studying, eating, and doing laundry—that may be the most difficult to manage. You may have made it through high school just fine with only an occasional glance at your planner, but in college, a good planning system is a fundamental survival tool. Your printed or electronic planner (e.g., PDA, phone, computer) will focus and track your daily and weekly schedule, and in doing so, will reflect your values, priorities, and resources.

How you keep track of everything is less important than actually keeping track of everything. If you poll your friends, you will find that some use a store bought planner, some use their cell phone calendar, and others use computer based calendars and then sync their calendars with their PDAs or cell phones. In deciding the best way to manage your schedule, remember this:
- The method must work for you.
- You must use your system consistently.

Skills Ahead

Regardless of the specific method, model, or tool for scheduling or managing your time, the common skills required in the scheduling process will make or break your ability to manage your time well. Consider those skills now:
- Setting priorities (master list)
- Creating a plan (weekly calendar)
- Forecasting events and anticipating problems (adapt)
- Making decisions (daily schedule)
- Committing to follow through (motivation/discipline)

Setting Priorities

The overriding influence in any schedule is priorities—determining those things that are most important and making sure they come before those that are less important. As you plan your days, your long-term priorities will quietly sit in the background, guiding the way you manage your daily schedule.

As he left the biology lab, Carl wondered, "Do I eat lunch, finish my reading for my afternoon class, or get the oil changed in my car?" Deciding what is most important and how you order your priorities, may not be as simple as it sounds. Carl's afternoon priorities are influenced by a deadline, a health issue, and preventative maintenance. His priorities will likely change with his circumstances. If he skipped breakfast and has classes scheduled into the evening, lunch may be the first priority. If he is responsible for leading a discussion, his reading may be the highest priority. If his car has an oil leak and he doesn't have oil on hand, the oil change may come first. While Carl will face different scheduling challenges tomorrow, by stepping back and setting priorities for the semester, month, and week, he establishes a foundation for the decisions he must make today, and the many new decisions he must make throughout the semester.

You and your classmates share a common goal—complete your degree. You will devote several years of your life and undertake significant expense to achieve that goal. Therefore, those things that you must do to successfully earn your degree are worthy of a spot at or near the top of your priority list.

If you are working to pay tuition, housing, or expenses or have been awarded an athletic or academic scholarship, your work or performance will be a priority, as each enables you to pursue your goal of higher education.

On graduation day, you and your classmates will join in celebrating your common achievement. But as you continue your journey to that day, you will face different opportunities and challenges, and thus have different priorities. With the overarching goal of earning your college degree, turn the page and complete your Goal Pyramid, identifying the other goals that will guide your time planning. Those goals may encompass a wide variety of areas, including income and performance goals.

Exercise 3.3 Goals

My Goal Pyramid

My Overarching Goal: Write the degree you plan to earn while in college on the line below.

_____

Take a few minutes and brainstorm to identify the smaller goals you must attain or steps you must take to earn your degree. List them in the bubbles below. (Your list of smaller goals might include declare a major, complete all of my general education classes, apply for a loan, register for classes each semester, work summers, work part time, find an internship, etc.)

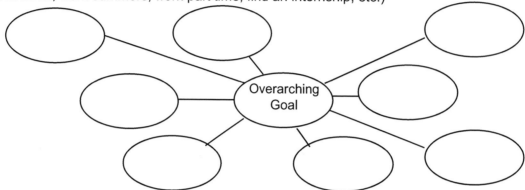

Now write your Overarching Goal at the top in the top block of the pyramid. Write your supporting goals in the smaller blocks of the pyramid, working up, with your most near term goals at the bottom. Arrange your supporting goals in the smaller blocks of the pyramid.

HINT:
Abbreviate your list of goals to single words.

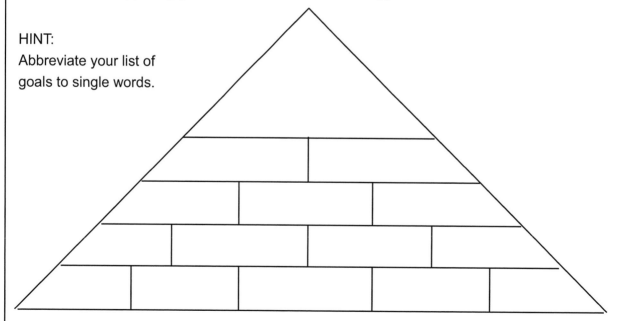

By looking at your pyramid, you can see that many short term goals will lead you to your degree. Understanding the place of each goal in your process of working toward your degree underscores the value of each step in the process and keeps you on track as you pursue your degree.

Stay on Course

Your overarching goal of earning a college degree acts as the ship that will carry you forward into life. The many other short-term goals that accompany your degree are the anchors that keep your ship from drifting off course and into dangerous waters. They will help you to identify and prioritize your daily tasks. With those goals as a starting point, go now to Exercise 3.4, the Master To-Do List, and record all of the jobs, tasks, projects, and "stuff" you need or want to accomplish. Your list may include attending classes, completing papers, exercising, working, studying, doing laundry, and more. As you make your list, break large projects down into smaller jobs or tasks that can be accomplished in one or two hours. List everything that you can think of that can, should, or must be accomplished within a defined period of time.   In most cases, this time period may be as short as a day or as long as a few weeks.

When your list is complete, determine which items absolutely must be done ("A" task), which should be done ("B" task), and which could be dropped or delayed indefinitely ("C" task) without adversely affecting you. Assigning a priority to each task will take a little practice. Think about how each task relates to the goals you wrote above. Use a pencil with a good eraser, and don't be afraid to change priorities! You will perfect your system with use.

Exercise 3.4: Master To-Do List

Master To Do List	Priority A, B. C	Date
1.		
2.		
3.		
4.		
5.		
6.		
7.		
8.		
9.		
10.		
11.		
12.		
13.		
14.		
15.		
16.		
17.		
18.		
19.		
20.		
21.		
22.		
23.		
24.		

Finally, go back to your list and assign deadlines for each item. Some deadlines will be hard and fast (finals week, term papers, class registration), and others will be arbitrary (get my hair cut, exercise, call a friend).

Take one more look at the tasks in your Master-To-Do List. Answer these questions:
- Is each one relevant?
- Do you see tasks that take you closer to your goal?
- Are those tasks your A and B tasks?

If you answered no to any of these questions, go back through your master list and change your priorities. Develop the habit of asking those questions as you make choices and decisions about how to use your time.

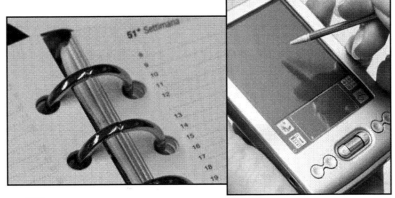

Creating a Plan

Planning your time is like planning anything: it must be intentional and is best done in writing. By writing out your plan, you will pull all of your best learning tools into the process, helping you to effectively weigh and process your options. You mentally repeat your tasks, make choices as you assign them dates and times, and create a visual representation of how your days, hours, and tasks are related.

Plan to manage your time by first laying out a weekly schedule, using the template provided or any printed or electronic calendar you prefer. A weekly schedule allows you to layout an optimum routine for your week. Once you have laid out one week, your other weeks will probably be similar. Weekly appointments or meetings; class, lab, and work hours; and set exercise times will take up about the same amount of time each week. Begin your schedule by writing those weekly events in the appropriate day and time block.

You have the basics of your week in hand. Be sure to look at your Master-To-Do List and add any important deadlines or tasks to accomplish this week. Consult this weekly schedule as you work in that extra movie, football game, concert, or study session. Make sure that you leave some margin—that is, a little time for unplanned activities—in your week.

Exercise 3.5: Weekly Schedule

Week: _____ to _____

Time	Sunday	Monday	Tuesday	Wednes-day	Thursday	Friday	Saturday
5:00							
6:00							
7:00							
8:00							
9:00							
10:00							
11:00							
12:00 Noon							
1:00							
2:00							
3:00							
4:00							
5:00							
6:00							
7:00							
8:00							
9:00							
10:00							
11:00							
12.00 Midnight							

Step back and look at the week you have planned, asking these questions and adjusting your schedule as required:

- Have I left enough time for necessary activities—sleeping and eating?
- Are all of my classes, work hours, and meetings included?
- Have I scheduled exercise times? Remember your brain works better when you exercise!
- Have I left appropriate study time? If you have not scheduled your study hours, do that now.

Tips for Planning Study Time

Number of hours:

The rule of thumb says, for every hour in class, you should spend two hours studying outside of class.

Variables in the equation:

The amount of study time required may vary depending upon these factors.

- Difficulty of the class
- Your reading efficiency
- Your effective use of study skills and tools
- How the course seems to fit into your long term goals

When to study:

You will learn more by spreading your studying throughout the term. Studying notes immediately following classes and labs will improve your understanding and recall. Reading assignments before class prepares you to be an active listener. Following these tips will help you avoid all night cramming, which is not an effective long-term learning strategy.

Forecasting Events and Anticipating Problems

Lists, schedules, and plans are great, but what happens when things fall apart? You get sick, your car breaks down, your hard drive crashes, or you get locked out of your room? Suddenly you must shift into hyper drive and become a problem solver—you must adapt. Schedules are not static, they are dynamic and to effectively manage your time, you must a) be aware of your options and b) be creative in your thinking.

Being aware of your options requires that you forecast or anticipate possible problems and have a general knowledge of university policies and support services, have a few willing friends, and possess the judgment to know when to seek help. Do you know how to contact security? Do you know the hours for the health center? Can you get a prescription filled? If you oversleep, can you get to class fast, contact another student for notes, or pick up the broadcast of the lecture? Thinking ahead and anticipating the unexpected may make the difference between shifting into fifth gear or giving up altogether when things go wrong.

Creative thinking requires that you know your priorities, consult your schedule, develop a support system, and decide what you can shift or eliminate. When there is no time for lunch, maybe you grab an apple, crackers, and a bottle of water on the run. When you fall behind in your readings, maybe you 1) cut out that movie or 2) work out for only a half hour instead of an hour. Can you go late to the soccer match? While everything is on the calendar for a reason, not all tasks are equal. Know your schedule and your priorities, and create workable options when needed.

Making Decisions

While not everyone writes out a daily list, most people find that they are more productive if they do just that—write a list of tasks to complete daily. You can write your list at the end or beginning of each day, depending on where it fits best into your schedule. While many items on your weekly calendar remain the same from week to week, your daily list may change dramatically from day to day (e.g., meet with my study group, pick up my parking pass, do my laundry, apply for international programs, and return library books). Ideally, your weekly calendar reminds you of the static items on your schedule—class schedule, work schedule, and weekly appointments—while your daily list integrates the tasks that tend to be moving targets into the more static structure of your weekly schedule. These tasks fill in the otherwise empty spaces on your calendar.

You will find daily to-do items by reviewing your Master-To-Do List or your calendar. While you will quickly memorize your weekly class schedule, your Daily-To-Do List requires daily attention. You will assess your commitments, look over required tasks, and determine priorities, deadlines, and time available. Whenever possible, keep your daily list to ten items or less. The exception will be the groups of small tasks that inevitably show up—e.g., return phone calls, send e-mails.

The objective when scheduling is to make time work for you. Some days, you will find extra time in your schedule, some days you will find it impossible to get everything done. Your job is to remain in control. Don't let the schedule defeat you—make it work for you! Move what you can without dropping priority items off into the abyss. With practice, you will know what items can be tossed, what can be moved, and what absolutely must be done now.

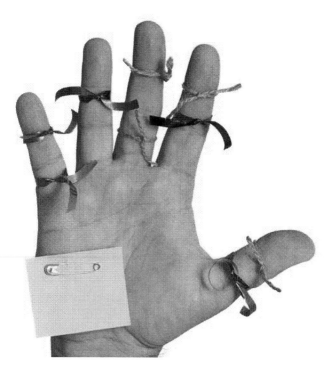

Reflection 3.6: Adapting My Schedule

Review the weekly schedule you just designed and ask yourself the following questions. As you answer each question, look for ways you can adjust your schedule or take other action to avoid problems.

1. What will I do if something goes wrong? _____
_____
_____

2. What is within my control and what is not? _____
_____
_____

3. Where will I go for help if I need it?" _____
_____
_____

4. Make note of important phone numbers and emails below. Then enter them in your phone or computer._____
_____
_____

Look back at your weekly schedule one more time. If every moment is taken, add "margins" now by taking a few lower priority items off of your plate.

Scheduling Tip

By keeping your life in order, you create room for a little disorder now and then. When opportunity knocks, and you are invited to go, do, or see something of interest, you will increase your ability to seize the moment if you have a clear picture of your available time and commitments.

Use the template that follows or the daily agenda you already use to make a plan for tomorrow. Remember to evaluate priorities, deadlines, and time available. Avoid more than ten items unless you are grouping small tasks (e.g., phone calls, emails).

Exercise 3.7: Daily-To-Do List

Name_____

Day_____   Date_____

Daily To Do List	Priority A, B, C
1.	
2.	
3.	
4.	
5.	
6.	
7.	
8.	
9.	
10.	

Overflow

Committing to Follow Through

Your goals are clear, priorities are established, and your schedule and to-do-lists are made. Now comes the magic of follow through—making choices that support your plan. Getting up on time generally requires going to bed on time; working out consistently may require accountability; and avoiding the black holes of technology—Facebook, texting, Twitter, e-mail, and latest Hollywood gossip—may require shutting down, turning off, or logging-out. Avoiding choices that derail your plan is essential to your success.

Planning to manage your time sets the stage to successfully accomplish your goals, but the plan is meaningless if you don't carry it out. Whether your plan is a nice idea or a road map to success will be determined in large measure by the approach you take to implementing your plan.

Money Talks

Think of your time plan as a budget. In this budget, time is the currency and tasks and responsibilities are grouped as debts, investments, or recreation. Just as not paying your financial debts results in penalties (e.g., discontinued services or finance charges) not making time for your tasks and responsibilities results in similar penalties (e.g., low grades or loss of jobs). In your time budget, tasks are the responsibilities that you owe to your future—school, work, scholarship requirements, and other goals or priorities. Debts, investments, and recreation should be planned around your responsibilities.

While your debts will drive most of your schedule, your investments should not be ignored. Like any good investor, invest for the long term, invest wisely, and make changes to your investments when necessary. These investments will be investments of time in relationships, health, and community, and while the return on these investments is not always measurable, it is very real. They fuel your personal growth, make a positive difference in the lives of others, and build your emotional, social, and physical health. When you move beyond college, those investments will be foundational to making the most of your academic achievements.

The defined deadlines of your courses and regular activities can cause you to feel boxed in by your busy college life. By deciding to make time in your schedule to enjoy the world around you, you create opportunities for mental and physical rest. Attending movies, going to plays, and taking vacations are examples of the recreational rewards you give yourself when you have completed your responsibilities and investments. The rewards can provide incentive to remain on your schedule and act as motivators as you plow through a busy week.

A time budget is a little different than a financial budget—the income is always the same— 168 hours per week. Because you can't earn more hours in a week, a time budget can quickly become over crowded. Avoid over commitment by including time cushions and back up plans in your schedule and using a time management system that you will employ consistently.

Back to the Beginning

Now that you have considered your priorities, developed a schedule, anticipated problems, made daily choices, and committed to real follow through, it is time for you to return to Reflection 3.2, which you completed on page 29. In the space below, write the areas you circled for possible improvement. Think about time planning tools and strategies that are described in this section, that you have used successfully before, or that someone has shared with you. Think of practical ways to improve one or more areas you identified in your reflection. Write those ideas next to the areas of improvement you wrote below.

Reflection 3.8: Improving Time Planning

Areas I want to improve:	Practical steps I can take to improve in this area:

Whether you began this section as a champion planner or as a novice in the field, you have considered and possibly shared many practical methods for gaining or keeping control of your time and your life. Now take everything to the next level and live it out in daily activities. Continue to be aware of how you spend your time and commit to keeping your time planning "budget" on track.

Tips for getting through difficult periods:

1. Look ahead: Anticipate particularly busy weeks. Whenever possible, complete readings and other assignments ahead of time.

2. Watch for big loads: Term papers, research, and other projects can be broken down into manageable pieces. Put each piece on the calendar in the weeks preceding the due dates and make every effort to meet your self-imposed "mini-deadlines."

3. Don't get caught at a dead end: Leaving every reading and assignment to the last minute leaves no room for error. If something comes up without warning, you may have to pass up a great opportunity, and you will have no room to accommodate unexpected requirements in your assignments. The stress of too much work and too little time is a perfect recipe for broken concentration and debilitating frustration.

Courage is
what it takes
to stand up
and speak;
courage is
also what it
takes to sit
down and
listen.

Winston
Churchill

listeningandtaking
noteslistening

listeningandtakingnote
noteslisteningandtaking

Case Study 4.1: Listening and Retaining

Eli's eyes flew open as he felt someone climb over his legs and head for the exit. For the third time that week, Eli had fallen asleep during the first half of his two-hour history lecture, jolting to attention only when his classmates headed for the door. Eli was embarrassed (hoped he hadn't gone so far as to snore or drool) and frustrated that he would once again leave class bewildered, lost, and confused. It wasn't that Dr. Right was boring, it was just that the combination of the large, warm lecture hall and the post-lunchtime energy drop were more conducive to a nap than to listening to a lecture.

Eli tried everything—recording lectures, drinking triple shot coffee, and taking furious notes. Recording lectures meant he had to go back and invest another two hours listening to the lecture he dozed through the first time. He thought a triple shot coffee would solve his problem, but after a few days, he was jittery, broke, and unable to concentrate. Desperate for a solution, Eli realized that the most successful students seemed to stay alert and take extensive notes throughout class. Unfortunately, his note taking efforts left him with cramped hands and a patchwork of notes, with too much information in some areas and not enough in others. In the end, Eli would give up and shortly thereafter, you guessed it—he was back to dozing.

Having exhausted all other options, Eli finally gave up and decided to make a visit to his professor during office hours. Feeling a bit embarrassed, he explained his problem. He was a little surprised when Dr. Right suggested that Eli's approach to learning was all wrong.

"I am not saying you can't learn," Dr. Right explained, "I am saying you don't seem to understand that your job for the next four years is to learn and to take learning seriously. It's not about finding some way to stay awake, it's about finding a way to understand and become interested in the subject being presented."

"I am sure you have heard the 'rumor' that for every hour you spend in class, you should spend two hours studying. That's more than a rumor, Eli, that is reality. So if you are in my class for two hours, what are you going to do for four hours outside of class?"

"Read my assignment?" Eli answered hopefully.

Without waiting for Eli to sort out other possible answers, Dr. Right pulled out a pencil and scratched a triangular shape he called an iceberg on his note pad. With a horizontal line cutting off the top fourth of the triangle, he explained that most of learning in college occurs in the bottom, underwater part of the triangle, the time outside of class. "In other words," he said, "real learning begins in the lecture hall, but it develops once you leave class and delve more deeply into the material. You need a guide through the deep waters, and that is me and the direction I have laid out for you in the course syllabus. So how do you get that direction?"

"From your lecture?" Eli ventured tentatively.

Dr. Right actually smiled and added, "and from the course syllabus! The secret to benefiting from the lecture is to listen actively. Active listeners do not doze or snore their way through my class. They actually find things pretty interesting. So young man, I want you to meet with Caren, the teaching assistant for this class. She is a pro at listening actively and taking notes effectively."

"I tried taking notes diligently, but nothing helped," Eli offered.

Dr. Right took another hard look at Eli and began to draw a curve on the back of his lecture page. "Eli, this is a forgetting curve. Look at the line. Within minutes of hearing a lecture, you have almost 100% recall – that is if you stay awake," the professor said, looking sideways with one raised eyebrow. Dr. Right continued, "But after twenty-four hours, your recall drops below 40% and after forty-eight hours, recall drops below 30%. Even if you stay awake and write every word down, by the next time you come to class, you are going to remember far less than half of the concepts, principles, and events I presented. How are you going to make sense of an entire course if you can't remember the last lecture?"

"Caren will explain the Cornell Note-taking Method and the best process for using notes to become an active listener. Follow the process, keep up with your reading assignments, and you will find that my history course is downright fascinating!"

While Eli appreciated Dr. Right's time, interest, and concern for his problem, he doubted he would ever use the word "fascinating" to describe the course. With his dad's words ringing in his ears— "You will get out of college what you put into it"—Eli set an appointment with Caren, learned to listen actively, and began to take Cornell notes, sometimes called two column notes. As the semester progressed, Eli remained alert and became a great listener—staying awake through every lecture—and a great note-taker—reviewing notes within twenty-four hours of every lecture.

Think it Over.

Who is responsible for Eli's learning? Who does Eli think is responsible for his learning? Before Eli went to see his professor, he tried to take responsibility for his learning by analyzing and solving his own problem. While Eli's efforts to take responsibility were well intentioned, were they effective?

Was Dr. Right interested in helping Eli? How can you tell? Would it be hard to go to a professor if you were in Eli's position? What did Eli learn from his visit to Dr. Right's office?

Do You Hear What I Hear?

The phrase "active listening" sounds good, but what does it mean? Active listening requires that you focus on the speaker and actually engage in a physical way with the message being presented. During conversation, these requirements are met by

- facing the speaker
- making eye contact
- nodding
- restating or asking questions

and a myriad of other visible and invisible reflective responses.

While the typical college lecture does not evoke a hearty "amen" or an enthusiastic "go for it!" an active listener will take a few important steps to ensure that he or she learns and retains the information presented.

Arrive early. Just as you face your friends during conversation and look for facial expressions and body position to reveal emotions, you will be a more effective active listener if you position yourself to notice body language cues from professors and other presenters. Begin active listening by arriving early enough to have a choice in seating. Plan ahead—beat the rush to class.

Sit where you can see and hear easily. Sit near the front and toward the middle, just like you would when attending a performance or concert. You will stay more actively engaged if you can see facial expressions and do not miss a note or lyric. *Listen* with your eyes by watching how your professor emphasizes key ideas through eye contact, hand gestures, and other forms of body language.

🎧 **Be prepared to consider what you already know.** If you have prior experience or knowledge regarding the topic being presented, tie new information to existing knowledge in your long-term memory. Make note of any key words or new vocabulary that may be used. Pave the way to better understand lectures by completing and taking notes on your assigned reading before arriving in class.

🎧 **Reflect back what you hear**. While your professor may not welcome your verbal agreement during the actual lecture, and time and class size may prohibit probing questions, your class notes will provide an avenue for reflection. Restate important points, write a question mark to indicate that clarification is needed, and summarize the big ideas. Sit forward and listen for the opportunity to reflect.

🎧 **Listen for the structure of the lecture.** While each professor will organize material in his or her own way, most lectures include an introduction, a body, and a conclusion. The introduction clearly presents the main idea of the lecture and may include why it is important. The body then presents a series of points with supporting information (illustrations, examples, data, clarifying statements). Finally, the conclusion ties everything together in one main idea or with a single thread. Find these three elements of the lecture as you write and organize your notes.

🎧 **Listen for verbal signals.** The average person speaks at a rate of about 125 words per minute, while the average person listens at a rate of about 500 words per minute. During lecture, your mind is moving at about four times the rate that the speaker is speaking. Where is your mind moving? Tame the wandering mind by challenging yourself to guess what is coming next and then questioning if you agree with the professor. Verbal cues will help you see relationships, identify main ideas, and predict what is coming next. Look for these words: "before I begin..., first..., next..., finally..., for example..., therefore..., on the other hand..., in contrast..., in summary..., in conclusion..."

Watch for graphic representations of ideas. Speakers often use pictures, diagrams, flow charts, and other graphic helps to reinforce and clarify concepts, ideas, and relationships. Pay close attention to each as you focus on understanding their use and meaning. Whenever possible, draw them into your notes. When viewing PowerPoint®, YouTube videos, or other computer or web-based presentation tools, note URLs, key words, or other reference data to locate the presentation after class. When instructors or professors make PowerPoint® presentation graphics programs available to you ahead of time, you may choose to type notes in the notes section below each slide during class.

Room for Improvement?

If you are actively engaged, listening can literally wear you out, but the pay off can be big for college students. Active listening during class alerts you to main ideas and important information and makes your study time more focused thereby saving you time as you prepare for any exams, papers, or projects that might be assigned. This cohesive approach to your learning will help to shift your new knowledge and understandings from your short-term memory to your long-term memory. Your active engagement reinforces all of your learning and gives your brain the

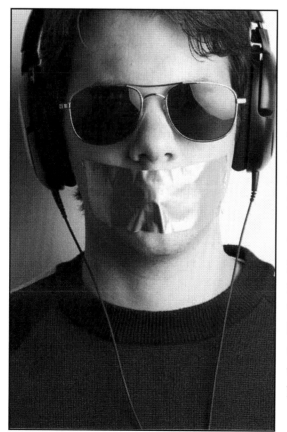

opportunity to do its best work. What's the pay off? When you begin to prepare for your midterm or final, many of the concepts, ideas, and information you are expected to know will be familiar and available for recall and use. Engage in active listening and you will save time, increase understanding, and improve performance.

Take a minute and reflect on the way you listen during lectures. How do you listen, take notes, and interact with the lecture? As you rate your listening habits, consider ways to expand your skills and habits and ways to use good listening skills and habits consistently.

Reflection 4.2: Active Listening Skills and Habits

I sit near the front and toward the center of the lecture hall or classroom.
- ☐ Always
- ☐ Usually
- ☐ Sometimes
- ☐ Never

I arrive for class
- ☐ Early
- ☐ On time
- ☐ Late
- ☐ Whenever

I complete my assigned reading before arriving for lecture.
- ☐ Always
- ☐ Usually
- ☐ Sometimes
- ☐ Never

I take interactive notes, identifying key ideas and any information that is unclear.
- ☐ Always
- ☐ Usually
- ☐ Sometimes
- ☐ Never

I stay awake in class.
- ☐ Always
- ☐ Usually
- ☐ Sometimes
- ☐ Never

I note the structure of the lecture in my notes: intro, main ideas, support and examples, and conclusion.
- ☐ Always
- ☐ Usually
- ☐ Sometimes
- ☐ Never

I watch for verbal and body language cues noting important information.
- ☐ Always
- ☐ Usually
- ☐ Sometimes
- ☐ Never

I copy and note any graphic illustrations.
- ☐ Always
- ☐ Usually
- ☐ Sometimes
- ☐ Never

Looking at the boxes you checked, would you say that you could improve your active listening skills and habits? Drawing from the previous reading or the questions above, identify one or more ideas that you would like to expand and incorporate in your own note-taking strategies. In the space below, write how you will incorporate the strategy, what benefit you expect from using the strategy, and when you will begin to use the new strategy.

_____

_____

_____

A Process and a Method

When Caren and Eli met to review Cornell note-taking, Eli was surprised at how very simple and straight forward the system appeared. While all note-taking encompasses writing down the key points, main ideas, and examples given during any presentation, the Cornell Note-taking Method and its simple three-step process is especially effective in higher education; the professor delivers or exposes students to knowledge and material, but students must take the initiative and provide the discipline to learn the depth and breadth of the subject.

Eli had taken notes in his more demanding high school classes, but had never experienced the fast paced, lengthy, and challenging lectures that he found delivered in college. Caren explained that it may be difficult to get all of the key points of every lecture written during class, but routinely using a simple system helps develop patterns and habits that improve efficiency and accuracy while allowing you to identify missing or confusing points.

Whether you have used Cornell notes throughout middle and high school or never heard of Cornell notes, take a few minutes to read or skim the next few pages; you may find a whole new system of note taking or simply learn adjustments you might make to your current method.

The Process

Dr. Right had it right when he explained the forgetting curve to Eli. Unless you review your notes, you are going to forget a significant portion of what you hear during class lectures. Any effective note-taking method will include a process to cover the time before, during, and after lecture.

 Before:

Arrive in class early enough to get a good seat. If you have not done so before arriving, take three to five minutes to review notes from the last lecture or two. What key ideas and illustrations have been presented? How will they relate to the topic about to be presented? Review key terms and vocabulary. Preparing your mind before lecture will increase your interest and alertness during the lecture.

 During:

Listen actively to the professor or instructor. Review the seven points of active listening presented on pages 48 - 50 and apply them during lecture. When determining what to include in your notes, follows these suggestions.

✓ Identify and write down key points and supporting information. Watch for items that are repeated or expanded.

✓ Terms, phrases, theories, and concepts that appear in writing—power point, overhead, slide—will be important. Highlight these in your notes.

✓ Be sure to mark (e.g., circle, star, underline, question mark) anything you don't understand for clarification later.

✓ Watch for examples and illustrations. Identify them under the points they support.

✓ Note pages numbers and all text references.

 After:

The lecture is over, but you will want to stay seated for one or two minutes, if possible. Quickly review your notes. Underline, highlight, or circle key points, write question marks where you need clarification, and fill in any missing information or note it for further follow up. If you have time and the professor is still around, you may be able to ask a question or two immediately following the lecture.

Within 24 hours, sit down and review your notes. In the Cornell cues column, write out vocabulary words, possible test questions, and important names, events, or theories. Look for connections between concepts, ideas, and examples. Finally, write a two or three sentence summary of the main sections of the lecture or the entire lecture. These cues and summaries, when well written, provide a great study tool for exams. This activity promotes the highest level of thinking—evaluating and synthesizing.

The Method

The Cornell Note-taking Method is widely used on college campuses. In its best form, the Cornell Method provides a pathway for moving information from your short-term memory to your long-term memory. In his book, *Brain Rules*, Dr. John Medina states that "The way to make long-term memory more reliable is to incorporate new information gradually and repeat it in timed intervals." [6] When applied consistently, the Cornell Note-taking Method helps make your long-term memory more reliable and eliminates the need for cramming—a very ineffective study strategy.

In this section, you will explore the basic appearance and use of Cornell notes. Unlike notes you may have taken on the back of an old handout, Cornell notes follow a specific format and are best written on a computer with good note taking software or on loose leaf notebook paper so that you can file your notes in order with course handouts and supplementary materials. Again, consider the way you handle notes and note-taking activities before, during, and after class.

The following guidelines assume that you are using paper and pencil for taking notes. If you prefer to use your computer or electronic device, apply these same guidelines to your electronic notes system. See page 62 for additional suggestions for electronic notes.

6   Medina, John. *Brain Rules, 147*. Seattle: Pear Press,2008. http://www.brainrules.net

Before:

Before you begin taking your notes, draw a vertical line on your paper about 2 ½ inches from the left hand side of the paper. Write the date of the lecture or discussion and the course or professor's name in the top right hand corner.

As you look at your paper, you will see two columns. The narrow column on the left is for your use during review after class.

The wide column on the right allows space for the notes you will take during class.

Narrow left column for review cues

Wide right column for notes during class

As you settle in to take your lecture notes, think about your role as an active listener.

- Choose a seat that allows you to see the speaker.
- Review previous notes and readings before the lecture begins.
- Reflect what is being said as you take your notes.
- Listen for structure.
- Consider verbal signals.
- Note any graphics.

During:

Take notes in the wide "notes" column with the above tasks in mind. Of course, note-taking in a fast paced lecture requires abbreviations, symbols, and shortened phrases. If you don't have time to write everything out, write enough words or symbols to allow you to complete that portion of your notes after class. For instance, identify examples with "EX." Use a basic outline format; separate main ideas, subordinate ideas, and supporting examples by indenting phrases or using bullets.

Write only on one side of the paper. This will allow you to lay out and see all of your notes when reviewing or looking for a specific lecture or key piece of information.

After and Beyond:

After class and whenever possible (but certainly within twenty-four hours, and absolutely no later than forty-eight hours) begin your review by reading the "notes" column out loud. In the small cues column, write the following information:

Possible test
questions

Important terms

Formulas

The narrow cues column will become a great test prep tool. When you are reviewing or studying for an exam, you can fold the 2 ½ inch cues column backward, turn the paper over, and use the questions and terms as a mini-quiz, with all answers hidden, but within easy reach if you get stuck.

Finally, at the end of your first review of your notes, write the summary of the material covered. In this summary, try to demonstrate a general understanding of the big ideas presented. Ask, what overarching ideas pull all the information together? This will help you draw connections between concepts, time periods, scientific discoveries, events, and outcomes. With greater understanding, smaller pieces begin to hang together much like the pieces of a puzzle.

	Susan Brown American History September 25, 2009
	Notes
	Native American Tribes
	1. Ancestral Pueblos
	Basic info
What region did the Puebloans live in and who are their descendents?	- desc. are Hopi, Zuni, and Pueblo tribes - lvd in 4 crnrs region of Southwest
	Mastery of Agriculture
	- manipltd h2o to grow crops
	- corn, squash, beans
What two things were the Puebloans most known for?	- very little game — hunt
	Housing/towns
	- made huge apmt like complexes
	- by 1200 BC moved — city to cliff
Pueblo = dwellings built into the cliff	dwelling — bc of Apache raids - 1,000 years later cliff pueblos disappear
	and NAs settle — New Mexico
	- sets stage – modern Pueblo culture
What led to the Ancestral Puebloans' downfall?	Downfall
	- vulner. to environment + hostile outside tribes
	2. Iroquois
	Basic Info

How many nations were in the Iroquois Nation? – look up names for correct spelling	- Lvd in reg. from the Atlantic to
	  Grt Lakes to So. Canada.
	- Iroquois Nation — 5 tribes, then 6
	  with reltd languages and cultures

	3. Mississippi Tribes
	Basic Info
	- villgs — from Illinois to the South
	- hunt, fish, raised corn
	Lrg Cities
What are three areas in which the Mississippi tribes rivaled European society?	- Kahoka – bigst city near St. Louis
	- At time, pop. was larger than all cities exc. Paris and London.
What is the evidence of a structured religious system?	- Rivaled European soc. in religion, trade, science
	- Religion – lrg burial mnds where religious leaders lvd
	- Trade – intricate trade routes — Kahoka ctr of
	- Tree arrangements like Stonehenge —arngd astronomically
What aspects of their geo-graphically regions did each tribe use to their advantage?	4. Common to three
	- Adptd strengths to environments
	- Pueblos – soc. related to agriculture — ahead of time
	- Iroquois – politically, used connctd tribes to frm internal and external militaries
	- Mississippi – used religious and scientific strengths
	5. Commonalities that led to conflict with Europe
How do Native Americans and Europeans differ on the idea of land ownership?	- Territorial – NAs and Europeans had different ideas of land ownership
	- Europeans exploited nat. rescs
	- Religion – zealous Spsh Catholic and Engl Puritans
Was conflict between Euro-peans and Native Americans inevitable?	The 3 highly advanced groups of the Puebloans, Iroquois and Mississippians used their geography to develop their strengths. Some of the same aspects were elements in each tribes conflict with Europeans.

Reflection 4.3: Note-taking

Describe your current note-taking method.

_____

_____

_____

_____

Identify aspects of the Cornell Method that you already use in your note-taking process.

_____

_____

_____

_____

Identify aspects of the Cornell Method or ideas you have observed or heard about from other students that you would like to begin to incorporate in your note-taking. Explain how each idea or strategy will improve your recall and/or understanding of information.

Ideas/strategies	Expected Improvement

Keys to Learning Supported by the Cornell Note-taking Method

1. Listen actively the first time.

2. Review immediately, accessing short-term memory before recall fades.

3. Review within twenty-four hours, reciting all information and distilling to main ideas.

4. Review all note cues weekly, using your summaries to trigger greater recall.

Cornell and Technology

While paper and pen notes have been the staple for generations of students, technology is the new player on the field, quickly becoming a favorite note-taking tool. While the ease of use and flexibility of hi-tech notes is appealing, ensuring that your electronic notes offer solid opportunities for recording, reviewing, and synthesizing the content in lectures is vital.

To reap the benefits of technology and Cornell note-taking, you will need an intentional system that preserves the basic principles of good note-taking.

1. **Power.** Begin by ensuring that your computer or other note-taking device has the battery power to last throughout your lecture or lectures. Switching systems in mid-lecture may be disruptive to those around you and will certainly be disruptive to you, so be a good scout, and be prepared.

2. **Fall Back Plan.** That said, being prepared includes a back-up plan—keep your trusty pen or pencil and paper handy in the event that your hi-tech gadget suddenly goes no-tech.

3. **Basic Note-taking Skills.** Once you are powered up, take your lecture notes in much the same way that you would on paper. Record key points, themes, terms, theories, phrases and concepts, using abbreviations and symbols when helpful. If you have strong keyboarding skills, abbreviations may actually slow you down. Adapt your system to make it work for you.

4. **Review.** Technology does not overcome the forgetting curve, so adding detail, reviewing, and summarizing your notes as soon as possible after class remains an important part of your learning. Add cues, questions, terms, and summaries in different colors or fonts, to allow for easy review later. If you intend to study and review your notes electronically, and can place two documents side-by-side for review, you may want to create a separate document to serve as the "cues" column and summary sections for your electronic Cornell notes.

5. **Adapting Printouts.** You may find that it is easiest to take and store notes electronically, but that the hard work of study and review requires the printed page. If you print your notes for review, be sure to leave ample margins for writing additional notes on each page. If you are going to store your printed notes in a three-ring binder, be sure to leave room for the holes on the left side of the page.

The worth of
a book is to
be measured
by what you
can carry
away from it.

James
Bryce

reading&retainingreading
&readingread
retaining&retainingread

Case Study 5.1: Reading for Understanding

It was a long week! Cameron took a major exam, wrote up a lab, and handed in her first college paper. While fighting a cold, she met all of her critical deadlines, but fell behind in reading for another class.

After dinner on Friday night, Cameron took hot tea to her room, closed the door, selected her favorite play list, and adjusted the light to shine directly on her books as she took her place on her bed to read. (Earlier in the day, Cameron promised herself that she would stay in for the evening and catch up on her readings.)

Fifteen text messages, thirty minutes, and four pages later, she realized she couldn't remember anything she had read. Frustrated, she turned off her cell phone and tried again. Soon she found herself dozing – another thirty minutes lost. It was now 8:30 on Friday night, the residence hall was quiet, and she was struggling to concentrate.

She called several friends to see if anyone else was studying, but found they were all out for the evening. Cameron kicked herself for falling behind in her reading, but putting the past aside, she remained determined to reach her goal.

With renewed commitment, she moved to her desk, got a fresh cup of tea, pulled out her pencils, and prepared to begin again. Remembering the methods she used during her hardest days in high school, she went back to the beginning of her text, read the introduction, scanned the headings, and looked over the charts, graphs and pictures. In only a few minutes, she found that her chapter was looking a lot more interesting. She pulled out her lecture notes and kept going.

Cameron stayed up late, finished her reading, went over to the student center, and ran into a few friends. After a few laughs, she returned to her room. Glad she had finished her readings, she went to bed vowing to plan a little better for her weeks ahead.

Think it Over

What was Cameron's goal for the evening? What contributed to Cameron's lack of concentration? Explain.

Cameron carefully chose her reading environment. What, if anything, would you suggest she do differently?

How did Cameron's environment affect her reading experience? Describe your "perfect" reading environment.

College Level Reading

College level readings present complex information, concepts, and principles. Cameron was not only fighting a long Friday night of reading, she was struggling with new vocabulary, dense text, and complex concepts. Seasoned college students realize that they must comprehend, use, and apply their "textbook" knowledge on many levels. Fortunately, research and experience has resulted in the development, publication, and use of many reading strategies for handling the volume and complexity of information college students must read and know within the various disciplines.

In this section, you will explore research-based reading strategies that will help you and students like Cameron successfully complete reading assignments. As you begin to understand and use different reading strategies, you will improve your effectiveness by adapting your strategies to your reading goals and expectations.

Variables

Before exploring those strategies, take a few minutes and consider the four variables involved in any effort to read effectively: students, text, strategy, and purpose[7].

---

7   King, Kathleen, Ph.D. "Reading Strategies." *Idaho State University.* 24 June 2009 <http://www.isu.edu/~kingkath/readstrt.html >.

- **Student:** Each student has a unique set of reading skills and interests as well as his or her own physical circumstances (e.g., fatigue, hunger). The study environment can be included as a factor in your physical circumstances (e.g., lighting, noise, seating).

- **Text:** Texts may vary in difficulty (e.g., easy and a quick-read or dense with text and information) and type (i.e., literature, science, math, humanities, social sciences).

- **Strategy:** Students must adapt their reading strategies to the types of text they are reading. When you use effective reading strategies, you can almost always successfully tackle even the most difficult assignments. Continuing to apply strategies will improve any student's reading skills.

- **Purpose:** When students understand the purpose of their readings, they must alter their reading strategies to match their purposes. Are you rereading to prepare for an exam? Are you pre-reading to prepare for a lecture? Are you reading to catch up? Are you reading to learn principles of engineering to complete a project?

Reading Strategies

Successful reading strategies are aligned with the way your brain processes and learns information. By thinking about the twelve brain rules published by Dr. Medina, you can predict some reading strategies that might prove effective. For example, Brain Rule number four states that we don't pay attention to boring things. Strategies to prevent boredom might include any activity or approach that helps the reader interact with the text: circling unfamiliar or key words, drawing a Venn diagram to compare ideas, writing questions that come to mind during reading.

Rule #1	Exercise promotes brain power.
Rule #2	The human brain evolved, too.
Rule #3	Every brain is wired differently.
Rule #4	We don't pay attention to boring things.
Rule #5	Repeat to remember.
Rule #6	Remember to repeat.
Rule #7	Sleep well, think well.
Rule #8	Stressed brains don't learn the same way.
Rule #9	Stimulate more of the senses.
Rule #10	Vision trumps all other senses.
Rule #11	Male and female brains are different.
Rule #12	We are powerful and natural explorers

Review the brain rules listed on the previous page and select two or three rules that could be used as a basis for a reading strategy. For each rule you select, write a specific strategy that you think might be incorporated in an effective reading experience.

Reflection 5. 2 The Brain and Reading Strategies

Rule # _____ could be the basis for this strategy:	Rule # _____ could be the basis for this strategy:	Rule # _____ could be the basis for this strategy:

SQR3

Now that you have taken a few minutes to think about how the brain works and what implications that has for reading, stop and consider one of the popular reading strategies many students use: SQR3. Whether you are familiar with this strategy or not, the acronym presents a simple, but descriptive overview of the process: Survey, Question, Read, Recite, and Review. Review the brief explanation of the five steps of SQR3 below.

- **Survey the chapter:** Create a big "picture" image of what you are about to read. Read the introduction; look at headings; skim key words, questions, and summaries. Plan your session.

- **Question:** Create and answer questions – Prepare your mind for what you will read by "waking" it up with questions. Ask, "What are main points, evidences, examples, and the relevancy to the rest of my reading and to the world? How might I use this in my life?"

- **Read the section:** This part of the strategy includes active reading, requiring that you make notes as you read and search for answers to the questions you wrote earlier.

- **Recite the main points:** Look away from the text and answer aloud the questions you wrote earlier.

- **Review:** Highlight or underline main points and add notes in the text or margin.

Effective and Logical

As you read through the SQR3 description, did you discover some of the strategies you predicted from Dr. Medina's brain rules? When you think about your past reading experiences, there is really nothing earth shaking in the SQR3 strategy – it is logical, it is aligned with how the brain works, it is not difficult to use, and it is easy to remember. So why is this system so widely used? It is widely used because it is effective and it is logical, is aligned with how the brain works, is not difficult to use, and is easy to remember!

Did you notice that when Cameron ran into her concentration problems, she fell back on the SQR3 strategies from her high school days? Any effective reading system will employ common researched-based strategies and then put them together in a method that is easy to employ. Once you have learned and applied these strategies in your own experience, you will find that you will use them for the rest of your life.

Throughout your high school years, you employed a variety of reading strategies. You may have used a system like SQR3, or you may have applied a series of strategies you developed through practical reading experiences. Whether you are a fast and effective reader or find reading to be a chore that you plod through, now is a good time to review the best reading strategies and methods used by college students, evaluate your personal reading strategies, and identify ways you might tweak or overhaul your own system. In this section, you will explore four key areas of effective textbook reading strategies:

Skills Ahead

- The three phases of reading a text book
- A discussion of common reading strategies
- Strategy adaptations for math and science texts
- Note-taking and annotation strategies

Three Phases of Reading a Textbook

Any textbook reading assignment can be broken into three simple phases:
pre-reading, active reading, and post-reading.

Pre-reading

Pre-reading prepares your mind to take in, sort, and categorize knowledge and understanding that you will gain from your reading. Just as you must set up and organize the files on your computer so that you can find your data later, you must mentally store and organize information from your reading in a meaningful way for later access and sorting. Pre-reading is the time to ask, "What is the big picture or big idea of this reading?"

Active Reading

Actively reading a textbook requires that you understand the complex concepts and ideas presented. As you read, you will make sense of new information by using all the cues within the text, accessing glossaries and dictionaries as necessary, and adjusting your reading strategies to the subject matter presented (math, science, literature, social sciences). Reading for understanding requires "active reading."

Post-reading

Post-reading combines strategies and tools that allow the reader to review, clarify, and assemble notes, facts, and concepts to reinforce the "big picture" or main idea of the reading. Summarizing information, reviewing your notes, and reciting them out loud or discussing them with others will help you connect meaning and understanding. Reviewing helps facilitate the recall of terms, facts, and main ideas. The greatest level of understanding will be attained in the post-reading phase.

Insight Tip

Effective use of reading strategies through all three textbook reading phases leads to synthesis, the highest level of cognitive learning. Synthesizing requires that readers stop and consider meaning in all phases of reading. In the post-reading phase, recombining or synthesizing all of the "pieces" to create a "whole" will challenge the reader to think beyond the words and ideas of the printed page and transfer understandings to new topics and disciplines.

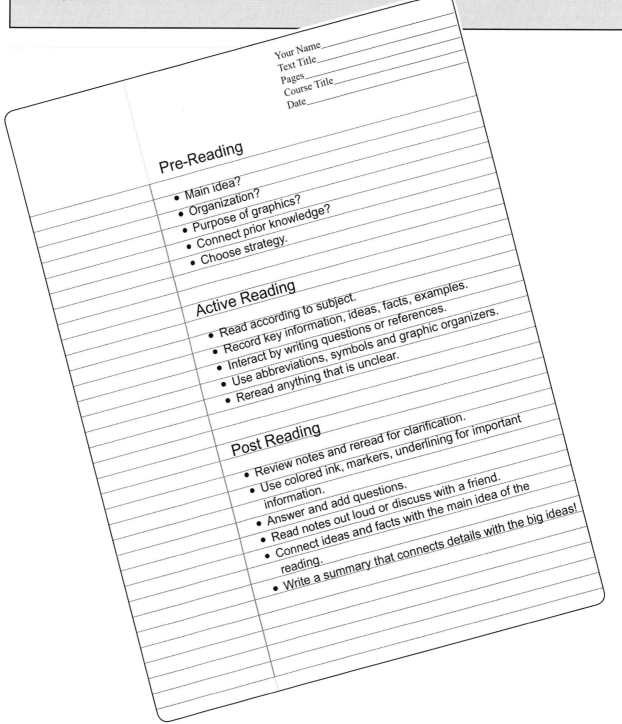

Your Name_____
Text Title_____
Pages_____
Course Title_____
Date_____

Pre-Reading

- Main idea?
- Organization?
- Purpose of graphics?
- Connect prior knowledge?
- Choose strategy.

Active Reading

- Read according to subject.
- Record key information, ideas, facts, examples.
- Interact by writing questions or references.
- Use abbreviations, symbols and graphic organizers.
- Reread anything that is unclear.

Post Reading

- Review notes and reread for clarification.
- Use colored ink, markers, underlining for important information.
- Answer and add questions.
- Read notes out loud or discuss with a friend.
- Connect ideas and facts with the main idea of the reading.
- Write a summary that connects details with the big ideas!

Choosing Strategies

Whether you know it or not, you have been using reading strategies—methods of improving reading and comprehension skills—since you first learned to read. You may have been taught very specific strategies, or you may have simply adopted other strategies as a result of reading practice and experience.

In the next few pages, you will find many common reading strategies described and arranged by each of the three reading phases. Although you have used many of these strategies in the past, you may increase your reading effectiveness or efficiency by using a familiar reading strategy in a new way or in a different phase of reading. Take a few minutes and read about each one, considering how you might use any of these to enhance your reading speed or comprehension.

Suggested Strategies for Pre-reading

Strategies that are well suited to pre-reading your text include:

- Read all front matter.
- Scan for organization.
- Read text questions.
- Locate and scan graphics.
- Consider prior knowledge.
- Know your purpose.

Read all front matter. When beginning to read a book, front matter may include a preface, table of contents, list of figures, opening statements, and more. Individual chapters and sections may include introductions. Other readings may include executive summaries or abstracts. Locate and read all of the relevant introductory material for the assigned reading. Use this material to provide cues to answer, "What is the main idea of this reading?"

Scan for organization. Scan the assigned pages, looking for the relationship between titles, section headers, and subtitles. Notice how the text is organized: chronologically, in stages, well known to little known, problems and solutions, cause and effect. As you understand how the material is organized, you will be prepared to move smoothly through the assignment; your mind will be ready for the next turn in the road.

Read text questions. Read all questions at the end of a section or chapter. Identify what you must learn and look for answers to final or summary questions.

Locate and scan graphics. Locate and scan all graphics and captions, including pictures, charts, examples, boxes, and graphs. Determine the purpose each serves in the text: interest, clarification, support, example, and evidence. Previewing the graphics may immediately reveal clarification or evidence for a key concept in the reading. Even in textbooks, a picture can be worth a thousand words and may save you time and frustration in understanding a complex concept. You may want to note and refer back to these visual and text helps at any point in your reading process.

Consider prior knowledge. As you begin to identify the main ideas, supporting information, examples, and other helps, stop and ask, "What do I already know about this topic?" Tying new ideas to familiar ones creates context or hooks for the new information you are about to learn. Facts and concepts from prior knowledge may be reinforced and recognized in the new text. Prior knowledge can provide the background required to gain insight into a new concept.

Know the purpose. Determine the purpose of your reading and then decide on a strategy for your reading that matches that purpose. Textbook reading strategies often serve one of two purposes: either preparing to hear a lecture or reinforcing or expanding upon the information already presented in a lecture. In math or science courses, the purpose may be expanded from learning the concept to being able to solve mathematical problems or to participating in a lab session. Most of the strategies presented here will apply to all of the above purposes. If you are reading to prepare for an exam, you will have already followed many of these strategies and may only need to skim the text and focus on that text which provides clarification or reinforcement of facts, concepts, and ideas. This idea is expanded in the test prep section beginning on page 105.

Reflection 5.3 What do you think?

Think about what you just read about strategies to use during pre-reading. In the spaces below, identify strategies you have used before, new strategies you would like to use, and strategies you would like to understand better. Describe when and how you might adapt these strategies in future assignments.

Pre-reading Strategies	Used Before	Like to Use	Understand
Read all front matter.			
Scan for organization			
Read text questions.			
Locate and scan graphics.			
Consider prior knowledge.			
Know the purpose.			

How I might adapt these strategies in future assignments

Suggested Strategies for Active Reading

Strategies that are well suited to actively reading your text include:

- Align approach with purpose.
- Adapt to the subject matter.
- Take notes.
- Annotate text.
- Identify vocabulary.
- Use organizers.
- Interact with questions.
- Reread.

Align approach with purpose. Align your approach to your reading with your purpose. If you are reading before or following lecture, read for depth of understanding using note-taking or annotation strategies. (See description and examples on 78 - 80.) If reviewing for an exam, scan the text for main ideas, important facts, and key graphics. Align your emphasis with your class syllabus or your professor's direction.

Adapt to the subject matter. Adapt your strategies to the subject matter. Reading for math and math-based sciences requires different strategies than reading for English or the humanities. While you may be able to read and scan English or history texts for main ideas, math texts demand that you read carefully, working all problems and examples. See the section, Strategy Adaptations for Math and Math-based Science Texts on page 77.

Take notes. Take notes on key ideas, concepts, facts, and examples. Use an outline format or simply identify key points and supporting information in a hierarchical manner. Record page numbers so that you can review or expand key points at a later date.

Annotate text. Annotate the text in the book with colored ink, pencil, markers and highlighting. While annotating draws your attention to specific material, if used randomly, annotating will become meaningless. Read an entire paragraph or section before underlining or highlighting. Mark only the main ideas or key points. Rule of thumb: Do not underline or highlight more than 50% of any text.

Identify vocabulary. Identify and define all special terms, vocabulary, and jargon. Use your glossary or dictionary and write all definitions within notes or on the textbook page.

Use organizers. Use abbreviations, symbols, and graphic organizers when appropriate. Commonly used graphic organizers include fish bone charts for cause and effect, Venn diagrams for contrast and compare, web charts for event mapping, pyramids for representing the main idea of a topic or key idea, circle charts showing stages in a process, tree charts showing main ideas and supporting details, and flow charts to show chronology. Remember the old saying, "A picture is worth a thousand words."

Interact with questions. Interact with the reading or your notes by writing questions or references to related concepts, ideas, or facts. Use the questions and related information to challenge your initial understanding and identify transferable knowledge that links your topic to broader or deeper applications.

Reread. Take time to reread any section that is unclear. You may choose to read aloud.

Reflection 5.4 What do you think?

Think about what you just read about strategies to use during the second reading phase. In the spaces below, identify strategies you have used before, new strategies you would like to use, and strategies you would like to understand better. Describe when and how you might adapt these strategies in future assignments.

Reading Strategies	Used Before	Like to Use	Understand
Align approach with purpose.			
Adapt to the subject matter.			
Take notes.			
Annotate text.			
Identify vocabulary.			
Use organizers.			
Interact with questions.			
Reread.			

How I might adapt these strategies to future assignments.

Suggested Strategies for Post-reading

Strategies that are well suited to post-reading include the following.

- Review your notes.
- Highlight the important.
- Answer questions.
- Read aloud.
- Integrate with the main idea.
- Summarize.

Review your notes. Fill in answers and expand notes to add clarity and understanding. Refer back to your text for further explanation as needed.

Highlight the important. Use colored ink, markers, and underlining to highlight information you may need to recall.

Answer questions. Answer the questions that you wrote during your reading. Record your answers in writing within your notes or speak the answers aloud.

Read aloud. Read your notes out loud or discuss them with a friend. The opportunity to say and hear the key ideas of your reading will help you identify connections in the text as well as missing information.

Integrate with the main idea. Ask, "How does this idea, formula, or information explain or fit with the main idea of the reading?" In this way, you will bring relevance and continuity to separate pieces of information.

Summarize. Write a short summary that emphasizes the connection between the details of your notes and the big picture of the reading.

> "Most textbooks now come with extensive support materials online. My most successful students have commented on the benefits of practice tests, crosswords, flashcards, and simulations provided on these sites."
>
> Dr. Rick Stewart, Ph.D
> Professor of Education

Reflection 5.5: What do you think?

Think about what you just read about strategies to use during the second reading phase. In the spaces below, identify strategies you have used before, new strategies you would like to use, and strategies you would like to understand better. Describe when and how you might adapt these strategies in future assignments.

Reading strategies	Used Before	Like to Use	Understand
Review your notes.			
Highlight the important.			
Answer questions.			
Read aloud.			
Integrate with the main idea.			
Summarize.			

Ways I might adapt these strategies to future assignments.

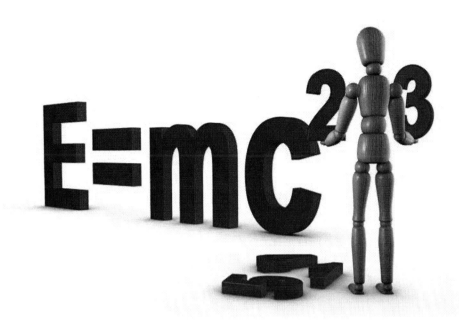

Strategy Adaptations for Math and Math-based Science Texts

As you practice and expand your reading strategies, you will begin to develop familiar patterns of reading. You will find that most literature, English, and social science texts can be read using similar or identical strategies. It is worth noting that math and math-based science books require that you make a few adaptations of your most commonly used strategies during the three phases of reading.

Math-based textbooks tend to have less words and more symbols than other texts, and therefore, require that you read deliberately, carefully defining all terms and jargon. Filled with theorems and sample problems, you should work each sample comparing your steps with those presented in the text.

While you may define vocabulary from contextual clues when reading in the humanities, mathematical terms must be precisely defined. Terms may define an operation or describe a process. Each new step is built on your understanding of the last. Precise language is required.

The practice exercises at the end of each section offer you an opportunity to repeat, practice, and apply the principles, theorems, and formulas just presented. Take advantage of these practices. Scan all problems, whether assigned or not. Work extra problems to help reinforce any area in which you need more practice.

As you work samples and reread instructions and formulas, you may find that you spend a half hour or more on a single page. It is important that you set your goals and adjust your time expectations according to these differences.

Reading Tips:

1. Plan your reading session, setting a specific reading goal for the time period you will read.
2. Read in fifty-minute blocks of time. Take a short break and get up and move around at the end of each block.
3. If you are having trouble concentrating for fifty minutes, take short breaks every twenty minutes or so. (Take deep breaths, walk around the library or room, and then resume.)
4. Rewrite difficult passages in your own words.

Note-taking and Annotation Examples

Taking notes and annotating the text enables you to be a more active reader and creates a record of the key information you will need to understand, apply, and recall. This section will provide examples of ways to effectively record notes and annotate text.

Annotation Sample

Annotating text can be a very effective strategy for engaging with the text on the page, but annotating is not about underlining and circling everything in the text that jumps out at you. A few tips will help you annotate a textbook purposefully.

After you have identified the main ideas of the text, set goals for your reading, and examined all graphics, you will be ready to find key information that supports the main ideas. Make annotations directly on your text pages during the second stage—active reading.

- Read each section or paragraph and ask, what is the main idea?
- What do I need to learn and remember? Is this an important example or illustration?
- Then underline, write a comment or question in the margin, or highlight words or terms you want to remember.

See Example 5.6 on page 79, which demonstrates how one student annotated the text from page 66 of this workbook.

Note-taking Sample

Many students use the Cornell Note-taking Method to organize their text notes. The two column format allows you to visually separate the body of your text notes from key ideas, vocabulary, and important questions. The summary section encourages you to restate the main ideas of the reading. Notice that this style of notes supports the reading strategies of the active and post reading phases. See Example 5.7 on page 80.

Example 5.6: Text Annotation (based on page 68)

Effective and Logical

simple,
logical

As you read through the SQR3 description, did you discover some of the strategies you predicted from Dr. Medina's brain rules? When you think about your past reading experiences, there is really nothing earth shaking in the SQR3 strategy – it is <u>logical,</u> it is aligned with <u>how the brain works,</u> it is <u>not difficult to use,</u> and it is <u>easy to remember.</u> So why is this system so widely used? It is widely used because it is effective and it is logical, is aligned with how the brain works, is not difficult to use, and is easy to remember!

Did you notice that when Cameron ran into her concentration problems, she fell back on her SQR3 strategies from her high school days? Any effective reading system will employ common researched-based strategies and then put them together in a method that is <u>easy to employ.</u> Once you have learned and applied these strategies in your own experience, you will find that you will use them for the rest of your life.

My Job:
review
evaluate
improve

Throughout your high school years, you employed a variety of reading strategies. You may have used a system like SQR3 or you may have applied a series of strategies you developed through practical reading experiences. Whether you are a fast and effective reader or find reading a chore that you plod through, now is a good time to review the <u>best reading strategies and</u> methods used by college students, <u>evaluate your personal reading strategies,</u> and <u>identify ways you might tweak or overhaul</u> your own system. In this section you will explore four key areas of effective textbook reading strategies:

Skills Ahead

Key areas

1. The <u>three phases</u> of reading a text book
2. A discussion of <u>common reading strategies</u>
3. Strategy <u>adaptations for math</u> and science texts
4. Note-taking and annotation strategies— *important*

Example 5.7: Sample Text Notes[8]

	Susan Brown 04/2/09 Psyc. 101
	Psychology Notes
	Chapter 8: Infancy and Childhood (contiuned) PP. 348 - 365
Ask mom or dad about my cognitive development, so I can have personal examples.	2. Preoperational stage – preschool to age 6 or 7. Still too young to perform mental operations
	- lack conservation – idea that volume, mass and quantity remain the same in different forms of the object
What are other examples of conservation?	Ex. The same amount of juice in different size cups
	- at this stage children are egocentric and can't see another's point of view p. 356
	- Piaget also came up with the theory of mind to describe when we can sense other's feelings, thoughts and predict behaviors, a skill children still lack in this stage p. 357-359
	3. Concrete Operational Stage – 6 or 7 to age 12 p. 360
	- begin to understand conservation and mathematical
An example of mathematical transformation – addition is understood before subtraction.	transformations
	- start to gain mental ability to think logically about concrete ideas
	4. Formal Operational Stage – starts at age 12 p. 263
	- now able to understand abstract ideas such as
What is the difference between concrete and abstract ideas?	hypothetical situations and consequences
	Reflecting on Piaget's Theory
	- Still some controversy over this theory, but worldwide tests show that babies develop the same despite cultural differences
	- He focused more on sequence than exact ages
	- Modern psychologists used Piaget's theories to develop new and more advanced theories
	There are three types of physical development: brain, motor and cognitive. Jean Piaget is the father of the theories of infant cognitive development. There are four stages: sensorimotor, preoperational, concrete operational, and formal operational. Each has a an approximate age attached to the stage.

---

8   Based on text from Meyers, David. *Exploring Psychology*, 6th ed., New York: Worth Publishers, (2005).

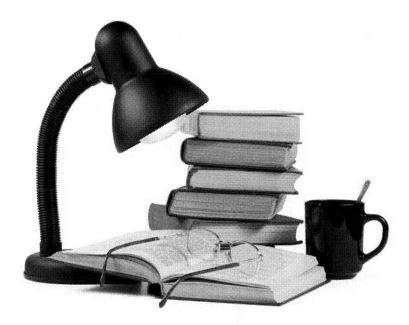

Making It Your Own

You have covered a lot of ground in the last few pages, reading about the many ways you can approach your college textbooks and meet the expectations of college level learning. It is time to think about your learning preferences, past reading experiences, and how you might integrate ideas to support your growth as an effective and efficient college student.

Complete Sections I and II of Reflection 5.8 to build a plan for your next reading assignment.

Reflection 5.8: Reading Strategies

Section I: Reading Phases

Select strategies you will use during each reading phase.

Pre-reading Strategies:

- ☐ Read all front matter.
- ☐ Scan for organization.
- ☐ Read text questions.
- ☐ Locate and scan graphics.

- ☐ Consider prior knowledge.
- ☐ Know the purpose.
- ☐ Other - describe. _____
  _____

Active Reading Strategies:

- ☐ Align approach with purpose.
- ☐ Adapt to the subject matter.
- ☐ Take notes.
- ☐ Annotate text.
- ☐ Identify vocabulary.

- ☐ Use organizers.
- ☐ Interact with questions.
- ☐ Reread.
- ☐ Other - describe. _____
  _____

Post-reading Strategies:

- ☐ Review your notes.
- ☐ Highlight the important.
- ☐ Answer questions.
- ☐ Read aloud.

- ☐ Integrate with the main idea.
- ☐ Summarize.
- ☐ Other - describe_____

_____

Section II : Reading Plan

In the space below, use an outline, a graphic model, or write a short essay to describe how you will use the strategies you selected above in your next reading assignment. Don't forget to adapt these strategies when reading a math-based text!

The best
helping hand
that you will
ever receive
is the one at
the end of
your own arm.

Fred
Dehner

writing&research
writing&research

Case Study 6.1: Electronic Woes

It had been a long month. Kane's research experience in high school was limited to two, five-page research papers and an 11th grade chemistry project, and now, only weeks into college, he was tasked with writing an eighteen- to twenty-page paper using at least fifteen sources. The mere thought of writing such a long paper had nearly launched a full blown panic attack, but instead, Kane had steeled his nerves and gone to the student support center for a little help. Now, Kane was in the home stretch. For nearly three weeks, he had been the last person out of the library. As the lights went dim, Kane would dash for the stairs and slip out the door as the library assistant impatiently waited, key in hand, to lock the door behind him.

More often than he wanted to admit, Kane followed his late nights in the library by working half-way through the night to complete more research and writing. Now, eight primary sources, nine secondary sources, and an eight-page annotated bibliography later, Kane was nearly finished with the second draft of his nineteen-page paper. Exhausted, but satisfied with his efforts, Kane shut-down his computer and went to bed for a much deserved night of sleep. Tomorrow he would ask Samantha, his faithful study partner, to proof read his paper. Unless she found some major problem with it, he felt confident that he could finish the final draft early the next evening and get a good night's sleep before the paper was due.

Kane got up early the next morning, turned on his computer, and headed for the shower.

As he towel dried his hair, Kane thought through his next steps; he would get dressed, do a quick read through of his paper, print it out, and grab a quick breakfast before heading to a full day of classes. He would meet with Samantha at lunch and leave the paper for her to review.

As Kane quickly entered his password, his computer screen suddenly went black. A powerful punch in the stomach would have been easier to take. Hoping for the best, Kane tried again – maybe this was just one of those quirky, high-tech moments. Kane turned on his computer, took a deep breath, typed in his password, and hit "enter." Like an airplane crashing to the ground, Kane's computer flashed an array of neon green letters and in a moment, all was black. With no back-up plan, Kane's weeks of work and diligent attention to the details of his assignment were suddenly gone.

Kane looked at the 20 GB flash drive that hung unused on a tether next to his desk. If only...... Kane recalled that his professor had warned students that they should back-up their work often, just in case something happened. Kane had been confident that his shiny new computer wouldn't let him down and had ignored his professor's warnings. Now feeling foolish, alone, and with no place to turn, Kane sunk into his chair. No amount of excuses and explaining would solve Kane's problem. Even if his professor took pity on him and gave him time for reconstruction, the workload ahead of him would not leave room for him to start over.

Eventually, Kane grudgingly accepted the painful reality that he had one day to reconstruct his weeks of effort. Fortunately, a few days earlier, Kane printed a partial copy of his rough draft. Knowing that he had an enormous challenge ahead of him, Kane made a plan to reschedule his day, rewrite his paper, and eventually, accepted the disappointment of being evaluated on a paper that was probably not going to be his best work. As he made his way to the door and toward breakfast, Kane vowed to get his flash drive off of the wall and into action, doing frequent back-ups of all of his work. Disappointed but not defeated, Kane was sure that this was one early college lesson that he would never forget!

Think it Over, Write it Out.

What did Kane do well in approaching his writing assignment? Why did he not back up his paper?

Once the computer had crashed, was there anything else he could do? What would you do in Kane's situation?

Has something like this ever happened to you? Explain.

Do you back up your computer work? What steps do you take to ensure you have easy access to your backup files in case your computer fails you?

Academic Writing

If undergraduate writing were a race, the exam essay would be the sprint, the persuasive essay would be the 400K, and the research paper would be the marathon. Just as sprints and marathons share many skills in common, essays and research papers share principles of good writing. Yet marathoners are not necessarily good sprinters and vice versa. All academic writing includes a few essential elements:

- Thesis statements

- Focused writing

- Clear organization

- Supporting examples or evidence

- Good mechanics

While expectations for test essays may vary due to time constraints imposed by the exam format, expectations for assigned essays and research papers will be unique, clear, and specific. These expectations may include length, tone, purpose, style, sources, and more.

In the end, while your specific writing tasks may vary, virtually all of the writing you do in college will share a common audience, the academic community—the community of students and scholars engaged in higher education and research. Throughout college, your writing will have to pass the academic "sniff" test—integrating solid knowledge and intellectual processing into your sound writing skills.

Collegiate and high school writing are built upon the same basic principles, but collegiate writing requires more complexity and therefore, more flexibility in thinking and approach. Opportunities for do-overs are not extended to the college student. You will be expected to turn in your best work the first time. Whether you are an experienced writer with highly developed skills or a struggling writer with growing skills, all student writing will be judged by the same standards, which are often more stringent, more clearly defined, and more strictly enforced than high school standards. In an effort to equip students to become respected thinkers and communicators, professors will critique the skills of even the strongest writers.

As a new college student, it is likely that you will be encouraged or required to take a college level writing class during your first or, perhaps, your second term. These classes reflect the need for you to know and follow the writing standards of your institution and your professors. With academic writing in mind, this section will

- review the basic writing process

- consider the role of research at the college level

- share helpful writing tips for students

In other words, this section will be a guide as you navigate the challenging waters of collegiate writing, refining and fine tuning your existing writing strengths. At the same time, this section is not a replacement for a collegiate writing course. If your honest appraisal of your own writing is that it is relatively weak, run, don't walk, to the nearest class, student support center, or resource program to get the help you need to begin to master this critical skill.

Revisiting the Familiar Writing Process

Some students can recite the writing process in their sleep and others—not so much. While the process may be described in as few as three and as many as six steps, in the end, it will encompass the following tasks:

- Pre-writing

- Writing

- Reviewing/revising

- Editing

- Publishing

Pre-writing

There are no short cuts to producing a quality college paper; however, a well traveled pre-writing process may prevent false starts and rabbit trails. Knowing where you are going and how you will get there, always saves time. Pre-writing is the warm up to your writing; attention to your pre-writing activities never wastes time—it establishes the purpose, direction, and depth of your paper and keeps you in the "zone" as you develop your argument or idea.

Topic. When you approach your assigned paper, commit to fully understand the topic of the paper. Whether you are assigned a topic or choose your own, exploring the topic carefully and defining the scope of your paper will lay the foundation for all that follows. Extremely narrow topics box you in, restricting thinking and research. Extremely broad topics leave you trying to drink from the proverbial fire hose—too much information and no way to absorb it. When considering and refining a topic, ask yourself several questions:

- What do I know about this topic?

- Why is this topic important and relevant to me?

- Is this topic of interest to my audience—the academic community?

- Will the length requirement of the paper allow me to fully explore the topic?

- Will the time allotted for preparation allow me to acquire and fully explore the resources necessary for developing the topic? (i.e., Is the topic better suited to a Ph.D. dissertation than a freshman term paper?)

- Are there credible and available resources that provide clear support for my main ideas, arguments, or conclusion?

- Can I find enough sources to be thorough in my research?

- Will I have time and substance to allow for making critical connections between the topic and my perspective or argument?

Purpose: While the purpose of all academic writing has been described by Karen Gocsik as presenting the "reader with an informed argument,"[9] distinct purposes can be further described as to persuade, explain, describe, or narrate. Keep the purpose of your paper clearly in front of you as you begin gathering and organizing resources.

Gather resources and organize thinking. During pre-writing, you will gather information about your topic, organize your paper, and write your thesis statement. Depending on the purpose of your paper, you may engage in interviewing, internet or library research, or brainstorming. Keep notes and a record of sources as you complete your research. You will find that graphic organizers and outlines will be a great help as you organize facts and ideas, structuring them in a manner that allows you to visually and thoughtfully analyze and evaluate before writing. (See sample organizers on page 90. See the College Research Writing section for further discussion – sources, note taking, and plagiarism.)

Your thesis statement presents the main idea and organization of your paper. Like a good road map, a good thesis statement will guide you as you plan, write, and review. As you work through the early stages of your writing, you may change your thesis to better reflect the findings of your research and the demands of the assignment. Early in your collegiate career, you may want to consult with professors or campus writing support services to ensure that your thesis meets the requirements of your assignment.

Tone, audience, and purpose. During pre-writing, you will consider the tone, audience, and purpose of your writing. The academic community usually expects a formal or semi-formal tone in your writing:

- Write in third person with precise word choice.

- Use action verbs; avoid passive voice construction.

- Avoid the use of jargon, slang, and abbreviations.

Don't confuse formal writing with boring writing; know your audience and write to develop strong interest, creative insights, and clear connections. Academicians are people, too. Speak to them! Having determined your purpose when you first refined your topic, consider it again as you develop your language and your argument or explanation. Ensure that your tone and language reflect your purpose in writing.

9   Gocsik, Karen. "What is an Academic Paper?" *Dartmouth Writing Program,* 10 July 2009. <http://www. dartmouth.edu/~writing/materials/student/ac_paper/what.shtml>.

Sample Graphic Organizers

Cause/effect

Subject:_____

Causes	Effects

Spider Map: Central idea and supporting information

Chain: Series of events in order

Time Line: Collect data for narratives or important events

1.

2.

3.

4.

Cluster Maps: Problem/solution

Parts of the Problem

Problem

Possible Solutions

Venn Diagram: Compare and contrast

5 W Questions: Collect details for narratives/stories

Who?	What?	Where?	When?	Why?

Graphic Tree: Depict hierarchical relationships

subject

main pt.   main pt.   main pt.

details details details details details details

Reflection 6.2: My Pre-writing Skills

Think about the pre-writing activities you have used when writing papers in the past and those discussed in the previous pages. Turn back to those pages, and underline ideas and tasks that may make your pre-writing efforts more effective. Take a few minutes to jot down several notes, outlining steps you can take that will make your next writing assignment clear, focused, and insightful.

Writing the Draft

Use all that you have accomplished during pre-writing to guide you as you write the first draft of your paper. Begin to write, freely flowing from one idea to the next, referring to your notes and outline or graphic organizer. While you may choose to develop your introduction after the main body of your paper is written, do not skip your thesis statement.

> **Let Your Thesis Be Your Guide**
> Write your thesis statement at the top of your first page and on a 3 X 5 inch card, referring to either or both whenever you need to regain focus.

Free Flowing

As in all good writing, construct well organized paragraphs—topic sentences, supporting detail, all tied back to the thesis—but don't get bogged down developing the "perfect" phrase, sentence, or paragraph during the first draft. Get everything down on paper now and in the next step—reviewing—you can revise, cut, rewrite, and enjoy seeing your well stated explanation, argument, or insights jump off of the page.

Perfect as You Go

While free writing may be the most common approach to academic writing, you may prefer another approach to writing your draft: write carefully and deliberately, fully developing each sentence and idea before you move on. While some students prefer this more "painstaking" method of writing, they may find that if they hit a road block, they have nowhere to go. Backing up and rewriting, or plowing ahead on an uncertain course may be their only choices. A carefully developed and elaborate outline may keep you on track and moving if you prefer the "perfect as you go" method.

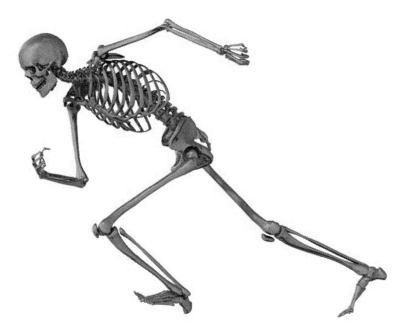

Reviewing/Revising

If you think of pre-writing as a skeleton and writing as "guts," you could then consider reviewing, editing, and publishing as the skin of your paper. The skin keeps the insides in place, allows the body to fulfill its function, and makes everything look better. Some of your most difficult work occurs in the reviewing/rewriting stage. You must step back from your paper and outside of your own thinking to ensure that your paper fulfills its purpose and meets all the standards and requirements of good writing.

> **Time Out!**
>
> Tackle reviewing after your draft sits for a while, otherwise you are simply reminding yourself of what you wrote, or intended to write, and will overlook obvious errors. Because you are reviewing for so many qualities at the same time, discipline yourself to review your paper several times limiting your scope each time you go through the paper.
>
> 1. First, read for organization and purpose, noting sentences and paragraphs that need to be revised, moved, or removed.
> 2. Reread for clarity and sentence structure.
> 3. Next read for grammar and mechanics.
> 4. Finally read for adherence to format guidelines and do a final proof of the paper to make sure you caught all errors and did not add typos in new or revised sections.
>
> NOTE: Make changes after each reading.

What Do You Think?

Peer reviews can be very helpful when writing especially complex papers. Remember that a peer review provides a third party opinion; be sure that you are not expecting a friend to rewrite your paper. It is up to you to accept and apply, or reject and ignore the suggestions. Keep a balance that will help you produce your best work. While it may be extremely humbling to have others slice and dice your writing, it is easier and wiser to let your ego take the hit early. Your ego will bounce back, but once the grade is given, it will stand.

If you are pressed for time, you will find yourself cutting short the review and revise phase of writing. While not ideal, you must do what you must do. However, if you dedicate yourself to learning from each paper you write, you will become a more efficient and effective writer, planning your time to allow a more thorough review of your work on each subsequent assignment.

You may find it helpful to complete your review tasks by answering a series of questions, such as those that follow, to address the six major traits of good writing. As you write for different professors and instructors, adapt this list to reflect their expectations and priorities.

Reflection 6.3: Review Checklist

Organization
- ☐ Is the thesis clearly stated or implied with specific details and language?
- ☐ Is your organization clear and effective?
- ☐ Does each paragraph enhance the thesis?
- ☐ Is the main idea of each paragraph well developed and supported by ideas or examples?
- ☐ Is the flow between sentences and paragraphs logical?
- ☐ Are the transitions from one idea to another clear and smooth?

Evidence and Attribution
- ☐ Is original thinking evident?
- ☐ Do you use relevant and convincing evidence and examples?
- ☐ Do you use quotations and paraphrasing effectively?
- ☐ Do you give proper attribution for quotations and paraphrased statements?

Introduction
- ☐ Do you use an interesting hook?
- ☐ Is your thesis well stated?

Conclusion
- ☐ Do you summarize the main idea or restate your thesis?
- ☐ Do you go beyond the thesis, broadening your conclusion to answer the question, "So what?" or validate your argument with a provocative quotation?

Mechanics
- ☐ Are sentences complete and well structured?
- ☐ Is punctuation used properly?
- ☐ Are quotations and paraphrased statements properly attributed?
- ☐ Check for:
    - Noun-verb agreement
    - Person
    - Spelling
    - Grammar usage
    - Word choice
    - Voice
    - Parallel construction

Format
- ☐ Do you follow the prescribed MLA, APA, BSE/CSE, Chicago Manual of Style, or other style requirements?

Editing/Proofing

Editing and proofing puts the polish on your work. Careful reviewing and revising leads to the final editing and proofing of each sentence, paragraph, and page. This is the stage at which typos and ambiguous sentences are found. Editing and proofing is the last chance to catch errors in mechanics. Allow time to put the window dressing on your well crafted paper.

Publish

Print or publish your paper according to your professor's or institution's guidelines. Professors may have their own preferences. Some may prefer to read your paper the old fashioned way, in hard copy. Others may ask you to turn it in in electronic form—on CD, flash drive, or by email. Still others may require a combination of forms (e.g., a printed copy and CD). Whatever they ask, be sure you are clear about the publication details and meet all the expectations.

The Research Paper

Nearly every student encounters the marathon, the research paper, sometime in the first year of college—often in the first term. The college research paper represents and makes visible the learning and thinking process that characterize college level learning. "Students develop understanding when they explain, when they apply knowledge to new problems or situations, when they develop an interpretation or perspective, when they analyze, when they evaluate, when they integrate and synthesize ideas."[10] These qualities come to life and are explored in the depth, breadth, and construction of the college research paper.

10   "Writing in the Major." *University of Wisconsin—La Crosse*. 10 July 2009. <http://www. uwlax.edu/wimp/teach/write4understanding.htm>.

As you proceed through the research process, you will actively read and record information, allowing you to explore the meaning of your topic as you explain, apply, evaluate, integrate, and synthesize ideas. Your final paper will reflect those activities, supporting your thesis with complex and well constructed arguments and explanations.

Sources

By definition, a research paper requires honest and extensive research of a topic. A skilled use and understanding of sources builds a foundation for original thinking that sets a final paper apart from the pack. With the ease of internet access and increasingly sophisticated search engines, you must resist the temptation to restrict your research to articles and materials readily available on the web. Although deadlines may make library research feel like a time drain, the quality and depth of sources found are worth the investment.

When looking for sources, remember to balance your findings between primary (first hand) and secondary (commentary) sources—both are valuable, but they are not equal. Primary resources may reflect the observations, perspectives, images, or biases of those present at the time of the event. Secondary resources reflect the interpretation and analysis that time and distance allow. Each serves a vital and unique role in understanding your topic and building your argument.

As you read, explain, interpret, analyze, and evaluate the information of various sources, you must consider the credibility of each source. Generally, publicly available online sources maybe more suspect than print sources, though all must be considered if you hope to produce valid and credible insights, comparisons, analyses, and evaluations. The validity of your original thinking requires that you consider these issues:

- Is the source backed by a well known institution or publisher?
- What is the reputation of the author?
- How credible are the links, references, or quotations within the source?
- Can the information be validated from another source?

To gain ready access to credible sources and some of the most current research in a particular field, you may want to use peer review journals and the online data bases made available through your college or university libraries.

Peer Review Journals

The concept and use of peer review journals may be new to the freshman student. This category of sources will save you time and ensure the credibility of the articles, data, and reports that you read and cite. Peer review journals are periodicals that publish only articles that have first been submitted to and reviewed by a panel of experts or scholars in the field. In addition to credible research, peer review articles often cite sources that will lead you to research you might have missed.

I tell my students that peer review journal articles sometimes contain statistical analyses that are difficult to understand, so as first year students, they may find it better to read the introduction, literature review, hypotheses, and conclusions sections and skim the results section if they don't know statistics.

The information in peer reviewed journals is on the cutting edge of new discoveries, debates and theory building in the social sciences and humanities. It may take months for this research to appear in a mainstream or popular publication... Professors are very impressed when first-year students delve into the world of academic journals. By your senior year, it will become a natural part of the research process.

Dr. Ken Waters, Ph.D.
Professor of Communication
Pepperdine University

Library Databases

Your college or university library will offer a variety of online databases to support your research. Stepping beyond the scope of most public libraries, these targeted databases often provide extensive and comprehensive access to resources. Experienced student researchers find that some of the most useful articles and research is available through the databases offered by their college libraries.

Research Tools for the College Research Paper

An annotated bibliography and systematic method for documenting notes and sources will assist in organizing the quantity and ensuring the quality of research that you must complete in preparing a college research paper. If you have successfully created annotated bibliographies and thoroughly documented large numbers of sources in the past, you may want to merely skim this section as a review, but if you have little experience with one or the other, take the time to thoroughly read and consider their use now.

Annotated Bibliography

Annotated bibliographies are often part of college research regardless of whether the research is finally reported or only discussed. Simply stated, an annotated bibliography performs three functions:

- Gives a listing of the sources (e.g., books, articles, documents, interviews, films) used for researching a topic.

- Provides one or more descriptive paragraphs for each source, thus the name "annotation."

- Presents an evaluation of the relevance and quality of each source.

Finding Sources

When researching your topic, another researcher's published, annotated bibliography may help you find sources you might otherwise overlook.

Like a good movie review, an annotated bibliography tells the who, what, where, and why of your sources. Be sure you understand your instructor's specific expectations in content and format; required elements might include a summary, assessment, or a reflection.

Summary:

You will describe the main argument or point of the source (thesis).

You may include hypotheses, proofs, and conclusions.

You will want to cover the scope of the work, including relevant topics or chapter titles.

Assessment:

You will evaluate the strengths and weaknesses of the source.

Consider reliability, objectivity, and usefulness of the source as it relates to your topic.

You may evaluate the authority and background of the author including biases, evidence, and other works.

When reviewing popular and professional journals, you might consider the intended audience.

Reflection:

Describe how you used this source. Explain the relevance of the work: Is the full work related to your topic, or are only selected sections pertinent? If your thinking changed as a result of reading this source, explain how. Explain if this resource affected the scope of your argument.

As an undergraduate student, an annotated bibliography will be a working record of the reference shelf you are building to develop and support your thesis. Completing thorough and thoughtful annotations of your potential sources will challenge you to think critically about the different sources and their relevance to your thesis, forcing you to go beyond simply collecting sources.

Annotated Bibliography Entries

Annotated bibliographical entries follow a specific format when required for an assignment. Follow the format prescribed by your instructor, department, or institution. All format requirements dictate that you record the bibliographical data according to one of several prescribed formats: APA, MLA, CBE/CSE, Chicago, etc. Include your annotations below your entry and use spacing and indents to offset the annotation. See the sample annotated entry that follows.

Flynn, T. (2006, April). A Delicate Equilibrium: Balancing Theory, Practice, and Outcomes. Journal of Public Relations Research, 18(2), 191-201.

In this article, Flynn discusses future research in the field of public relations. He specifically mentions two areas of study. The first area is the balanced zone model, which uses several communication theories to study public relations. The second is an outcome-based model of public relations. Flynn argues that public relations practitioners and scholars face the challenge of demonstrating the outcomes and relationships that a public relations firm facilitates for organizations. He discusses the importance of quantifying and qualifying public relation efforts to determine how effective they are in achieving the goals and enhancing the reputation of an organization.

This article suggests that to balance the interests and needs of different parties, the public relations field needs to look at several dimensions and perspectives where communication between multiple stakeholders and stake seekers occurs simultaneously. Flynn argues that it is the scholars' responsibility to create methods that measure the direct or indirect outcomes of public relations divisions, especially with regard to the overall reputation of an organization. With new methods and a balance of theory and practicality, organizations will be able to clearly see the effects of public relations efforts.

Flynn's article is a very helpful source because it validates my hypothesis that organizations, especially smaller companies, are unaware of the full benefits of their public relations departments. The article specifically addresses reputation enhancement, which will provide evidence for my sub-point about the effects of subtle reputation enhancement. After reading this article, I realize I need to focus more on scholars and their contribution to public relations.

Keeping Everything in Its Place

The bigger the research assignment, the more information and the greater the number of sources you will handle. Whether you are searching for relevant sources, developing key points for your outline, considering precise language for your thesis, developing support for an argument, finding appropriate examples and quotations, or reviewing your notes, you will be going back to your sources over and over throughout your research process. The question is, can you find the source itself and can you locate the specific information you need? A thorough system for taking notes and recording source data is critical to your process. Take a few minutes and explore two methods for record keeping: paper and electronic.

Note Cards: Creating Paper Records

Note cards may be the answer to all of your record keeping problems. With a pen and good set of three by five cards, you can create a system to manage almost any undergraduate research project.

1. Create a bibliography card for each source: Record all basic bibliographical information for that source on that card.
2. Assign a number for each source and write it in the top left hand corner of your bibliographical source card. To make later citations and references easier, write the source number on each notecard from that source.
3. As you actively read your source, take notes on blank cards. Title each card according to the ideas, information, and examples you are recording.
4. Write the page numbers of the source on each card. This will allow you to find information, quotes, examples, charts, and any other data you might want to cite or refer to as you develop your paper and prepare you citations.

This simple system will allow you to flip through cards to find data, information, and examples at a glance. You can verify the accuracy of your recall as you write supporting arguments—names and other facts will be literally at your fingertips. Creating your annotated bibliography, regular bibliography, or works cited will be a snap. Using file cards is a simple, but effective way to handle the complexity of the college research project, but if you prefer an electronic system—read on!

Creating Electronic Research Records

Using the same principles and targeting the same objectives as the file card system, create a series of word processing files to record your research notes and sources.

1. Always create a dedicated folder for each research project.

2. Record all bibliographical information for all sources in a single file with a recognizable name. This will serve as your working bibliography.

3. Number each resource in the working bibliography. Order does not matter since the numbers will serve simply to link your notes to the corresponding source. When you complete your works cited or bibliography pages, you will follow the order prescribed by the assigned style format.

4. Create a single file for each source and record your source notes there. Name the file so that you can easily identify the source without opening the document. Differentiate between quotes and notes. Be sure to write page numbers so you can locate the information for review and give complete information when quoting. Avoid wholesale copying from electronic sources. Pick and choose pertinent information.

5. If you take some notes on paper, transfer them to your electronic files as soon as possible. Stray note papers may be easily lost and forgotten.

6. ALWAYS BACK UP YOUR FILES. Use a flash drive, a CD, or even an online service

Electronic records may seem quick to create and easy to locate. Used effectively, they may indeed greatly improve the speed and accuracy of your research and recording efforts. However, using an electronic system requires consistency and awareness on your part. First, you must have a computer or other digital recording device with you to record your notes when doing research. Next, you must discipline yourself to use the filing system you have set up or you will spend more time searching for notes than creating them, and finally, you must back up your work on an external drive or service or literally, all may be lost!

College research requires diligence throughout your research and writing process. Choose the system of documentation that works best for you.

Plagiarism

Plagiarism is of great concern in the digital age, and with good reason—any writer with a computer and internet access can copy whole documents with a single click. But plagiarism has been around since words have been in written form. While you would not think of stealing someone else's car, your strongest temptation to throw your integrity under the bus may be with regard to the written word. Plagiarism, using or imitating the words or ideas of others and calling them your own, is the cardinal sin of writing. While plagiarism is not a crime, it is a compromise of integrity that your college and your professors will not tolerate. Students who are caught trying to pass off the work of others as their own will generally find severe consequences await them, including a failing grade on an assignment, removal from a class, or even expulsion from school.

There are obvious plagiarism mine fields that you must avoid, including buying an essay or research paper from another student or online. Some instances of plagiarism are quite unintentional as one professor describes: "Once students have read the words of others on their topic, it seems near impossible for them to sort out their own thoughts from those 'so eloquently' said by others." But beyond the actual words of another, the idea or unique way of stating a thought may be protected. Even when paraphrasing, you might find yourself actually changing only a few words and therefore, still be plagiarizing another's work.

At other times, it can be hard to know if a piece of information is the unique property of others or factual knowledge, and therefore free for use without attribution to a source. The term *common knowledge*, when used in the context of plagiarism, refers to the assertion that facts and ideas that are commonly known do not need to be documented.

Take time to read and understand plagiarism as defined in your institution's code of conduct. Remember, plagiarism can be unintentional. A variety of web-based tools are now available to professors, allowing them to quickly confirm the authenticity of your writing. Be wise and don't let your real learning, authentic efforts, and great future be compromised by plagiarism. Be vigilant in citing sources and developing original thought whenever possible. When in doubt, err on the side of caution and attribute the words or ideas of others to their sources.

Common Style and Format Standards

MLA - Modern Language Association
For disciplines in the humanitites

APA – American Psychological Association
Natural and social sciences, economics, business, criminology

CBE – Council of Biology Editors **CSE** – Council of Science Editors
Plant sciences, zoology, microbiology, and many medical sciences

---

When solving problems, dig at the roots instead of just hacking at the leaves.

Anthony J. D'Angelo

Case Study 7.1: A War Zone

Sasha's sister Marina had left home weeks ago. With her computer bag over one shoulder and her Blackberry in hand, Marina waved to Sasha as she headed out the door, promising to be back in a few months. They had both heard tales of the war zone, but undaunted by the challenge, Marina was excited, and she assured Sasha that she was up to the task. Now, Sasha was beginning to wonder.

Sasha began to be concerned when after one week, Marina sent no word. After three weeks, Sasha tried to call, but Marina's Blackberry was out of range.   Sasha grew increasingly unsettled, as text messages went unanswered and e-mails floated through cyberspace. Finally after four weeks, a short message came through, "Rough time. Help found. Will call next week. Don't worry."

After six weeks and no further word, Sasha was at her wit's end. "Don't worry," she repeated. "Right, Marina!" she said out loud as she closed her suitcase and headed for the door. She jumped into her jeep and headed out to find her sister. Arriving at the airport, Sasha checked in and boarded the flight, determined to ensure that Marina was safe. As she transferred flights in the early morning hours, she became more and more fearful of the road ahead. How would she track down her sister?

After transferring to an airplane one might generously call a puddle jumper, Sasha was tired, sore, and hungry. Arriving in the little airport, Sasha grabbed her bag, fought her way through the local crowds, and wiped the sweat from her forehead and chin. Soaring temperatures and high humidity—Sasha could have sworn she was in a sauna.

Finally, she flagged down a bus and was on the last leg of the trip to find Marina. This is where the trail could grow cold. The bus dropped her at a large gate after dark. Peering past the gatehouse, she feared the treachery her sister had entered.

Trudging up the slope, she entered the barracks style building where Sasha had supposedly been stationed. The walk, the halls, and the rooms were littered with torn papers, ancient books, and abandoned computers. Cups and plates were sitting on desks, beds overturned. Sasha's fear for her sister mounted with each step.

Standing by the window, she spied one lone building in the distance. All light's blazing, the structure was a hive of activity. Holding tight to her can of mace and reaching for her flashlight, she moved silently through the jungle of tall trees and thick underbrush. As she approached the lighted structure, her heart raced and her palms grew sweaty. Obviously, this was an interrogation facility and detainees were being held against their will.

Fearful of what she might find, Sasha carefully pulled the old door open, only to be accosted by three young men trying to make there way into the fresh air. "Excuse me," one said. "May I help you?"

With all the courage she could muster Sasha replied, "Yes, I have come for Marina Keller."

"No problem! I can take you right to her. Just follow me." With a quick turn he was back through the door and before she knew it, Sasha was embracing Marina.

"Marina, I have been so worried," cried Sasha.

"I can see that," responded Marina. "Is that the mace I gave you last Christmas? Don't you remember that I gave you my schedule when I left home? Did you get my text?" Sasha nodded sheepishly. "Things are a little hectic here right now with midterms and all. Practically the whole school is studying day and night, but I have my last midterm in the morning. So come to my room, you can sleep while I study, and we'll catch up after my exam."

Walking arm in arm to the dorms, Sasha took a minute to admire the beautiful college campus in the middle of the moonlit night.

Think it Over

Obviously, this spoof exaggerates the stress of testing weeks, but the reality is that testing can come off as a carefully planned ballet or a treacherous war zone. Take a few minutes to think about what makes the difference between smooth sailing and chaos.

Do your exams feel more like a harsh interrogation for which any answer will be the wrong answer? Do you feel chained to your books and notes?

How do you prepare for exams? How far ahead do you begin to study? Do you study in different ways for different types of exams (e.g., multiple choice, oral, essay)?

Exam are stressful for all students, but for some, exams produce genuine test anxiety. How does preparation for an exam help to increase or decrease test anxiety?

Prepare and Practice Along the Way

How you feel about your studies will color the way you see everything around you. If you are anxious and unsure, you will begin to feel more like a prisoner than an independent student.

Sometime during your first weeks of college, you will face your first exam. Whether you face that exam with dread or simply feeling slightly anxious will be determined by your approach to your studies. Like a good athlete, if you have prepared and practiced regularly, you will look forward to the test of your skill. Even with good preparation, there will be times that, when pitted against a tough opponent or a difficult class, you may feel more than a little anxious. In all cases, focus, discipline, and good habits will help you win the day.

Approaching your studies with the skills and disciplines described earlier in this workbook will help you prepare for exams by ensuring that you learn and practice recall of your course material long before the exam. Managing your time, actively listening, taking and reviewing class notes, and reading and comprehending text assignments will spread your learning over each term. This facilitates the transfer of information from short-term to long-term memory, keeping it readily available for recall.

From the Beginning

Keeping up with college classes can leave you a little breathless, but getting behind can leave you dead in the water. Professors of college courses typically expect that you will take lecture notes during each class, read 100 or more pages weekly, and complete at least two major exams or papers during the term. Multiply that load by the number of courses you are taking, and you will begin to get a realistic picture of what just "keeping up" requires.

Keep in mind that if you are a full-time student, your weekly combined class and study time will be about the same as a full-time, forty-hour-per-week job. While most college courses are designed to be rigorous, your workload will be manageable if you attend all classes regularly and complete your assignments weekly. Getting a few hours behind for a week or two can turn what should be a forty hour week into a sixty hour week. After a couple of sixty hour weeks, you may lose your energy and enthusiasm for studying and face a disheartening uphill battle when preparing for exams. Take it from veteran students—life will be happier if you stay on top of your studies from the first day of class.

Look at a quick review of what a well disciplined student expects to achieve each and every week in each and every class:

- Complete assigned readings and notes before class.

- Review previous class notes just before the next class begins.

- Engage in active listening using Cornell or another note-taking method.

- Complete a quick end-of-class review.

- Thoroughly review notes and write cues and summaries within 24 hours.

- Complete the incremental tasks required for completion of papers, projects, and other long-term assignments.

Keeping up with these tasks ensures that you are learning systematically. With each new concept, principle, or set of facts, you are building deeper understandings by connecting previous knowledge and higher order thinking. Such discipline lays a solid foundation, which is likely to prepare you to perform well on your exams.

An Exam Overview

Your previous twelve years of exam experience have ranged from drawing circles around shapes to writing U.S. history essays or solving calculus problems; college exams are generally more demanding than even the most rigorous high school exams. With perhaps only two or three exams in a term, each covering massive amounts of information, you may quickly feel overwhelmed and buried by the work and time that exam preparation requires. The next few pages will be a guide as you prepare for your early college exams. Take time to consider what you may already know about test taking strategies that might streamline your studying, and file away a few new tips for your future.

Most colleges publish midterm and final exam schedules, so you may be facing several exams within days or even hours of each other. Carefully planning your time will be critical in such circumstances. Check your syllabi and enter all of your scheduled exams on your calendar now. If exams are rescheduled, immediately note the changes. Write your exam dates below and transfer them to your personal planner or calendar .

Exercise 7.2: Exam Schedule

Classes	Mid-term	Final	Other

As you prepare for your next exam, be sure to consult and annotate your monthly and weekly schedule. If you have kept up with your assignments, you might begin your dedicated exam prep two or three weeks prior to the exam, especially if you are preparing for exams in multiple classes at the same time.

Efficiency: A Word to the Wise

Improve your study efficiency by studying your most difficult material when you are most alert. Whenever possible, study during daylight hours (and early evening) and use your nights for sleeping. Effectively managing your study schedule includes allowing for adequate sleep. Your brain will retain information better and will reward you by providing better recall during exams and other high pressure moments.

Research Note:

Loss of sleep hurts attention, executive function, working memory, mood, quantitative skills, logical reasoning, and even motor dexterity.

Dr. Medina, *Brain Rules. www.brainrules.net*

While what and how you study are critical, where you study will also impact the effectiveness and efficiency of your studying. Working with your iPod dangling from your ears, your door open, cell phone vibrating, computer windows open with abandon, and two IM message windows going is not conducive to studying. Be honest—this is not multitasking, it is multi-distracting! Do yourself a favor and find a place to study that invites steady concentration. Some students choose a quiet spot in the campus library, find a remote corner in an alternate library, seek a secluded space under a tree, or leave campus to find a coffee shop where they will not run into friends and find themselves on an unplanned tangent. Take control of the crazy world around you by choosing where and how you study. Find a spot that works best for you and use it—often.

Tools of the Trade

You recorded your exam date, you have chosen when and where to study, but do you have the tools that will help make your study time hum like a well tuned engine? Good news— the tools that you need to prepare for any exam are the outcomes of the consistent study habits you are already practicing:

- Text and lecture outlines
- Text and lecture notes and summaries
- Flashcards
- Checklists of facts
- Cues sections of Cornell notes

How you use these tools will depend on your learning and study method preferences. If you find visual cues most helpful, you might choose to mark notes and flash cards with diagrams and colored pens, taking extra time to study all graphic representations. If auditory cues trigger better understanding and memory, spend extra time reading key concepts aloud and discussing concepts with your peers one-on-one or during group study, or with a T.A. or instructor. If you learn best from tactile cues, you might choose to walk around as you study notes or record and listen to summaries while you exercise.

The Power of One: Independent Study

If you prefer to study independently, begin by planning your study days and times leading up to each exam. Review your calendar, identifying the best days and times to schedule your exam prep. Create a study plan by determining the topic and amount of time you will study that topic. Create time blocks in your calendar and enter the topics for each study block. Set study goals for each session and note them on the calendar next to each study entry. Include the reading assignments and lectures notes you will review. Look over the time and review the tasks. Have you allotted enough time to review all that you need to before the exam? If not, adjust your calendar. Be honest, be realistic, and keep your study appointments. At the end of each study session compare ,your goals with what you accomplished. If you need to adjust your plan, do it right away, adapting and moving low priority tasks as needed.

Start with the big picture: If you have been writing weekly summaries of your readings and lectures, group them by topic and review each group, taking time to note anything you don't understand, have forgotten, or that must be memorized verbatim. Mark key information with highlighting, bolding, or underlining.

Narrow your focus: Fold back the cues section within your sets of class notes or print the cues file from your electronic notes. Review all your questions, terms, and facts. Ask the possible test questions from the cues, looking up answers as needed, using both your full notes and your textbooks. Go through your paper or electronic flash cards, reading each aloud and answering aloud. Create multiple groups for continued review: those that you know well, those that you sort of know, and those that you don't know at all. Review the second and third groups—those you don't know well—periodically throughout the days ahead.

Practice: As you continue to review, write more possible test questions. Continue to answer each question orally and in writing. To prepare for possible essay questions, create outlines with your main idea, key points and supporting data, information, or examples clearly identified. Get together with other students for practice as time and opportunity allows.

The Needs of the Many: Group Study

Many students prefer to study with others. They find that the commitment to study with others helps them meet their study schedules. They benefit by learning new study techniques; gaining greater insight into the instructor's perspective, emphasis, and goals; improving their recall by practice quizzing with others; and, as an added bonus, enjoying the company of the group.

Trial Run. If you have never or don't usually enjoy studying with a group, set up a trial run. Ask a group of no more than five or six students to join you for a study session. Set a date, time, and place for a first meeting; this is everyone's chance to determine if the group studies well together. At the end of your initial session, if everyone is in agreement, you can set up future study times. If not, everyone can go his or her own way, a little more experienced—having had an opportunity to collaborate on a plan of study.

Agenda. When planning the study session, be sure to set an agenda or time plan, and distribute it to each person. Advance planning allows everyone to come prepared with all study materials in hand, making the session more productive. Assign a specific amount of time for each task. An ideal plan might include the following activities:

- Compare notes on all lectures and summaries of reading assignments.
- Ask open ended questions of others in the group.
- Take turns asking questions and explaining concepts using cues from notes and flash cards.
- Brainstorm a bank of possible test questions for continued study.

Time Table. Set a time table that will work for everyone and give the group enough experience together to decide if future meetings will prove beneficial. You will need at least an hour to have any meaningful interaction, but may want to keep the session under two hours to avoid dragging out a difficult situation. Even if you decide to continue meeting together, you will learn and recall information better if all who are involved study on their own between group study sessions.

Think now about the ways you can incorporate your preferred styles of learning into the way you will adapt the study suggestions presented in this section. Write a brief paragraph describing how you can better use your daily study habits and preferred learning styles, and where you can study to make your studying and preparing for exams more efficient.

Reflection 7.3: Study Choices

Reflection 7.4: Individual or Group

Create a plan now for either independent study or group study. Answer these questions as you write your plan.

Independent study:
- When will you study?
- What will you study?
- How will you know that you are prepared?

Group Study:
- Who will you invite?
- When will you meet?
- What studying will you complete to prepare for the first session?
- After the study session, how will you study to ensure that you are ready for the next session?

Ready for Anything: General Reminders for Your Exam Day

- ☐ Get a good night's sleep.
- ☐ Arrive in the exam room early.
- ☐ Bring everything you need: pens, pencils, calculator, etc.
- ☐ Listen to all instructions carefully.
- ☐ Read all directions for each section of the exam.
- ☐ Make a time plan for each section of the exam.
- ☐ Answer the questions you know best first.
- ☐ Reading through the entire exam may give you clues to difficult questions or items.
- ☐ Look at both sides of each page to ensure you have not overlooked any items.

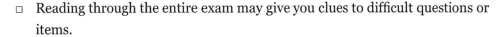

Practice for the End Game

While studying for an exam requires that you review and recall a mixture of facts and concepts, the type of test you will be given may dictate how you spend the greatest number of your study hours.

Prepare for essay exams by thoroughly reviewing your understanding of major concepts, events, and supporting evidence.

Prepare for objective exams by studying and memorizing facts, details, and definitions.

Prepare for a mixed exam, one comprising both objective items and essay questions, by identifying concepts and events that lend themselves to essay writing and facts and details that make excellent multiple choice, true/false, or matching items. Study each with the anticipated type of test question in mind.

- What will be on the test?
- What are the important ideas and facts?
- What connections must be made between concepts, events, etc.?
- How will the important information be tested?

Tips for Specific Testing Formats

While surprises are nice for birthdays, no one appreciates big surprises on exam day. High school teachers may give a complete breakdown of numbers and types of questions, but college professors may not share the same level of exam detail. While it is helpful to know the kind of exam for which you are preparing, thorough and consistent studying will help you prepare for any type of exam. That said, consider a few of the testing formats you may encounter and tips to assist you in studying and performing well on your exams.

Essay Questions

Essay questions are used frequently in college exams. Essay questions may seem more daunting than simple objective multiple choice questions, but essays play an important role in college assessment. Learning at the college level requires broad and deep understanding of material, often involving analysis, synthesis, and evaluation—the attributes of higher order thinking. Essay questions allow you to demonstrate that thinking. When a professor or instructor announces the essay format for any exam, you know that beyond facts, your main ideas and themes must include evidence of critical thinking.

What Did You Say?

Enumerate...summarize...compare...contrast...interpret...explain...analyze...prove...and the list goes on. Essay questions pose a specific question the student must answer. Before you can answer the question, you must identify the task you are expected to complete in your answer. Many of the task words are clear and concise: list, outline, summarize. Other words must be examined by their definition and in the context of the question: analyze, compare, contrast. Some words require simple statements or descriptions of facts, others may require analysis, synthesis, and/or opinion.

Task words. Begin by ensuring that you understand the task word itself. While you have encountered many of these words in high school and college prep exams, the college exam essay often hinges on the precise understanding of the word. Do not confuse similar words: contrast is different than compare. Take time to read and think about the similarities and differences between task words. Here are a few task verbs you should know well:

   Analyze: to examine closely by dividing the whole into parts, considering the relationships among the parts, and then describing how they are related.

Compare: to discuss the similarities between two or more objects, ideas, events, etc.

Contrast: to discuss the differences between two or more things, ideas, events, etc.

Criticize/critique: to judge and evaluate the worth of something giving evidence to support your perspective. Analysis is often a part of the critique.

Define: to give a clear and exact meaning for the thing being defined. Definitions are usually short, but are often used to explore other topics further. Definitions might be general in meaning or be specific to the course.

Describe: to give a verbal and detailed account of something often considering various characteristics and attributes. Can be in narrative form.

Discuss: usually involves a judgment made by considering the pros and cons of the subject or answering critical questions raised when closely examining the event, issue, etc. This task may include debate, compare, and contrast.

Evaluate: to make a judgment about something. Focus on the importance of the thing being evaluated by considering a standard or measured effectiveness of a thing. Present evidence.

Examine: to look closely at a subject, often analyzing details and implications of the investigation.

Explain: to make clear the details of a thing through a logical argument often focusing on the how and why of something. The explanation may involve reconciling differences in evidence or perspectives.

Illustrate: to show one or more examples, making the concept or meaning of an abstract point clear.

Interpret: to clarify or explain by making a judgment or considering a perspective.

Justify: to give a reason why certain decisions, actions, or conclusions are made.

Prove: to give a fact- and evidence-based logical argument.

Relate: to show the relationship, association, or connection between ideas or concepts.

Summarize: to describe something briefly, including key points and omitting details.

Trace: to describe the sequence, history, or progression of something.

Content. The next step to understanding the question is to determine the content that you are to address as you answer the question. Key content words will tell you what you are to write about. To find the content, ask the question "what?" after the task word. For instance, ask "Analyze or interpret what?" The answer to that question will be the content, topic, or scope of the question.

Focus. Once you have identified the task and content of your essay, you need to know the focus or limitations of the essay. The focus or limiting words will tell you what to concentrate your efforts on and may limit the time and resources you use. Look at the example of a simple essay question with all three types of words defined: task, content, and focus.

> "Compare and contrast the ethical problem solving models of Kant, Aristotle, Bok, Potter and Rawls (or others that have caught your fancy). Which one (or combination of ones) do you use most often when you are faced with communication issues that have ethical implications?"

In this sample, the task words are "compare and contrast." The content words (answering the question, compare and contrast what?) are "the ethical problem solving models." The focus is on five authors: Kant, Aristotle, Bok, Potter and Rawls.

Five Steps for Writing Exam Essays

Read before writing. Read all essay questions before you begin to write. If you are given the option to choose which question(s) you will answer, select the ones for which you are best prepared.

Answer the Question. The verb used in the essay question tasks you with a job that you must complete. An important rule in all test taking remains central to the essay exam: read the question carefully. You may want to underline key words and tasks. Understand what the question asks, and then, answer that very question and answer all points of the question. A great answer to a question that wasn't asked is still wrong and can mean a score of zero.

Outline and Structure. After reading the question, create an outline. Be sure your outline includes an introduction and summary as bookends to your key points and supporting information. Acting as your guide, an outline allows you to write faster and ensures that you include all the information in your plan. The outline forms the structure of your essay, which in turn makes your ideas clear to the reader.

Remember your essay answer must include and make visible higher order thinking. Burying important facts, details, or support in the wrong paragraph may indicate confusion and lack of understanding of the material.

Write the Essay. When you begin writing, keep your writing focused and get to the point. You may want to begin by rewriting a portion of the question or problem in your opening line. Stick with the organization you laid out in your outline. Write at least one paragraph for each of the following: the introduction, each main point you will be making and supporting, and your conclusion.

Review the Essay. If you have time, go back and read your essay, correcting grammar, spelling, and legibility. While you may not always have time, this valuable step is often the spit and polish an essay needs.

Testing and Time Tips

Before the test begins, decide how much time you will spend on each section or question. Jot those time targets in the margins or on an extra piece of paper.

Answer easy questions first. When you go back and begin answering the more difficult questions, mark any that you are unsure of so that you can revisit them at the end of the exam. (Sometimes other questions prompt you to remember key points related to previous items.)

Leave space between essay questions; you may think of something to add later in the period.

Keep moving. If you have time at the end of the testing period, go back and read over any questions you left blank, review answers you are unsure of, and add to or clarify essays if needed. Note: Often the first answer you thought was correct is indeed correct. Change answers only if you are confident in your new answer or certain your original answer is incorrect.

Multiple Choice

Multiple choice tests might be considered a mixed bag by some students. On one hand, each test item contains at least one correct choice, even if that choice is "none of the above." On the other hand, because multiple choices tests have so many questions, they often require that you are familiar with a broader range of topics than an essay exam. Each test item is worth fewer points than a single essay question, relieving some of the worry over wrong answers. Often, multiple choice questions offer detailed choices of names, dates, and definitions. Some of the tips for multiple choice exams involve ambiguity; multiple choice exams can be difficult to write, therefore, watching for errors such as noun and verb agreement may give you clues to wrong answers.

Tips for answering multiple choice test items:

- ☐ Before you read your choices, read the main question and try to answer without looking.
- ☐ If you are having trouble with the question, rephrase it in your own words.
- ☐ Do not guess if there is a penalty for wrong answers.
- ☐ Guess if you do not know the answer and there is no penalty for wrong answers.

True/false

You have been taking true/false tests since elementary school. Yes, the subject matter is more difficult, but in any true/false question item, only two choices are given. This format of testing usually assesses your mastery of details rather than general concepts. Review common tips for true/false items. Some professors will ask you to explain why a statement is true or false. This additional requirement raises the bar on the level of understanding you must demonstrate in a true/false statement. Always study as if you must explain why any statement is true or false.

- ☐ If part of the statement is false, the entire statement is false.
- ☐ Exams usually present more true than false statements.
- ☐ Statements with qualifiers like always, never, and only tend to be false.
- ☐ Statements with the qualifiers "often" and "frequently" tend to be true.

Matching

Matching sections require that you know almost all of the facts being tested. If you are well prepared for the material tested in the matching section, this portion of your exam will go quickly. Follow these tips to keep from running into rough waters when matching lists of facts and terms.

Read over the entire section to understand your choices. This is especially helpful when there will be items left over (i.e., in lists that are uneven).

- ☐ Match the items you know best first.
- ☐ Cross out the used answers as you go.

Reflection 7.5: Putting It to the Test

Consider all that you have read in this section. Consider the ways you are preparing for your exams and summarize your planning in the following chart.

My Class	Types of Qs on the Exam (if you know)	Ways to Prepare	The Tools I Will Use
	☐ essay ☐ multiple choice ☐ T/F ☐ matching other:		
	☐ essay ☐ multiple choice ☐ T/F ☐ matching other:		
	☐ essay ☐ multiple choice ☐ T/F ☐ matching other:		
	☐ essay ☐ multiple choice ☐ T/F ☐ matching other:		

With the End in Mind

Just like any athlete must train regularly before achieving the fitness and skill level required to play at the collegiate level, students must plan their study activities with the final acquisition of knowledge, skills, and applicability in mind.   Since the moment you decided to attend college, you knew that exams would be part of the package. What you may not have known or understood, was that those exams would come somewhat infrequently, and that they would often be the entire basis for your grades. That reality will be less daunting over time, as you refine your study and test prep skills, and become more adept at understanding your professor's expectations. You can remove much of the mystery from your exams by faithfully employing your good study habits; regularly monitoring course requirements, deadlines, and expectations; and intentionally using the test taking skills described in this section. You may never look forward to exams, but you might just find great satisfaction in seeing your hard work come back to you as personal success on your exams.

When
opportunity
doesn't knock,
build a door.

Milton
Berle

Beyond the Books

College offers a vibrant culture well beyond academics. Students from across the country and across the world create a kaleidoscope of cultures right within the confines of your campus. These strangers are now your peers—classmates, teammates, and, in many cases, these interesting students are your new friends. So how do you meet, get to know, and build friendships with the strangers all around you?

College Is What You Make It

Fortunately, your campus experience is already designed to build relationships—you are in a community of students who eat, learn, and often live together. Living in dorms, eating in cafeterias and campus cafes, and attending classes regularly puts you in each other's paths. In addition to those common daily tasks, you will find many optional activities to join—clubs, sororities, fraternities, sports teams, intramural teams, outdoor recreation, and campus entertainment. Opportunities to take part in off-campus activities may include camping, skiing, sightseeing, hiking, and attending plays, symphonies, and other fine arts presentations that you and your friends may enjoy.

Waves of Change

As inviting as all of these activities may sound, you will have to step outside of yourself to enjoy their benefits. Depending on your personality and past experiences, that may be easier said than done. If you have an outgoing personality and are comfortable in new situations, joining a group of strangers in a rock climbing excursion may be as easy as, well—falling off a rock. However, if you are a little reserved or not comfortable stepping into unknown territory, just saying hello to a stranger in a crowd may be a challenge. You can help yourself overcome your hesitancy to step out and join in by remembering that you and your fellow students are in this together. A quick scan of your freshman classmates will reveal that everyone is immersed in the same tidal wave of change. Those around you are also anxious to become comfortable and have a sense of belonging in their new college home, so you will find fertile ground for making new friends and connecting with others who share your interests.

Beyond your room, suite, or hall-mates and classmates, you will find others who share common interests when you choose activities, clubs, or events that interest you. As you step out on the intramural playing field, you will join others who share an interest in being active and maybe a little competitive. As you meet and get to know students in an activity of common interest, you allow for conversation and familiarity to grow in a natural setting.

Consider the opportunities on your campus. What groups or activities interest you? Have you inquired about, signed up for, or attended events, meetings, or activities? Find out when the next meeting or event will be held and make an effort to be there. Your Resident Assistant, student life office, school newspaper, school website, student activities center, and other students will be great sources of information. In the box below, create a list of events, activities, or clubs in which you have an interest.

Reflection 8.1: Group and Activity Interests

Money Talk

The issue of money is never far from the minds of most students. While the fixed costs of college—tuition, fees, housing, books—are officially addressed in your registration process, you are on your own when it comes to managing your daily expenses. In your new college culture, you are surrounded by students with a wide range of financial means. Some students will have virtually no extra spending money, while others may spend freely on food, entertainment, and personal shopping. Learning to share life with your new friends will include the need to respect one another's financial means, and when possible, to adapt your entertainment and activities to allow everyone to participate. If you find yourself with very limited resources, guard against the temptation to keep up with your more affluent friends by creating a financial crisis for yourself. If you have more disposable income than most of your peers, be sensitive to their financial constraints and choose opportunities that will not force them to choose between being left out and being tapped out. College campuses offer a wealth of free activities and entertainment that can keep your social life active and your finances in good health.

Eating out (i.e., paying for food and beverages not included in your meal plan) is one of the fastest ways to watch your bank account evaporate. While the campus cuisine may leave something to be desired, it comes at no additional cost to you and leaves your disposable income free for more exciting opportunities.

Finally, if you haven't done so already, be sure that you and your parents are very clear about the contributions they will make to your personal expenses. You and they will appreciate the clear expectations that you share, and you can avoid surprises and disappointments that can hinder those relationships.

Making Residence Hall Living a Positive Experience

Residence halls bring students together in an "up close and personal" way. Whether you live in a shared room in a suite or on a hall, or have a single room of your own, residence hall life means togetherness. Rules will be in place, courtesies will be encouraged, and group living will be experienced by all. You may be rooming with a friend or acquaintance, with someone you've conversed with briefly in phone calls or emails over the summer, or with a complete stranger. Whatever your situation, living with others is always a challenge.

Start off on the right foot by respecting your roommate's differences and individual needs. While roommates may share many common habits and interests, differences are bound to arise—adaptability is vital. Even opposites can live together successfully, but will always require an extra dose of mutual effort and understanding. In truth, almost every successful living situation requires effort and respect; it just seems a little easier to appreciate and make allowances for someone you understand.

Cleanliness Is Next to ...

Perhaps no single factor will contribute more to peace and harmony than keeping your room clean. While you don't have to stand ready for a white glove inspection, remember that your dirty socks, smelly gym clothes, and petrified snack remains are likely to be offensive to others. A clean living area is the easiest kindness you can extend to a roommate and includes the personal bonus that you are better organized. That organization will save you countless hours of playing hide and seek with your own belongings, will improve your time management and reduce your stress. In the end, you and your roommate will be happier if you keep your living place tidy.

If you and your roommate are adept at solving problems and extending courtesies, you will get through most of the year with little conflict. However, it is rare that a student can completely avoid a few rocky moments with friends or living mates. While college life is exciting, the new expectations and unfamiliar surroundings create more stress than most students realize; some of that stress is bound to be expressed in the "privacy" of your own room.

If you and your roommate are struggling to make life work in your little world (considering the size of the average shared room, "little" may be an understatement), assume the best about your mutual intentions and make an effort to talk through any difficulties that arise. Avoid walking away in anger and sleeping on the floor of another student's room. While that may seem to be a quick fix, it creates an entirely new set of problems that may be more difficult to overcome than the initial problem.

Resident advisors and other student life personnel are available to help you work through what may seem like an impossible situation. The simple suggestions below may help you take steps to demonstrate respect, find solutions, and set comfortable boundaries before tensions spiral out of control in areas of potential conflict.

- Speak openly.
- Use "I sentences."
- Focus on the problem not the person.
- Listen carefully.
- Be open to creative solutions.
- Maintain a calm demeanor and voice.
- Express and receive respect.

Remember, while you don't have to go it alone, be careful about talking with mutual friends regarding your roommate conflicts. By placing others in the middle of your disputes, you compel them to choose sides and build walls that may remain in place long after the real problem is resolved. Misunderstandings or disagreements can be easily blown out of proportion when you begin to rally a team to your side. Be the problem solver.

Who would you go to if you needed help working through a problem with someone in your residence hall? _____

Professors: Not Just Teachers

Beyond the new relationships you build through your living situation, activities, and other areas of campus life, you will be forming new and significant relationships with your professors and instructors. While you will not be living with your faculty, you will be spending a great deal of time listening to and discussing information with them. As authors of your courses, these educators will direct your learning and create expectations that may cause more than a little stress in your academic life. Students are often late in their college careers before they appreciate that the faculty that holds power over their grades also holds power to enrich their college experiences. Their years of experience working in their fields, collaborating with other professionals, and working with students equip your course faculty to support you in countless ways. By grabbing hold of that understanding early, you will create opportunities for clarification of material, assignments, or expectations, and begin to build relationships that will broaden your world and may later open unexpected doors of opportunity.

Professors post their office hours with the expectation that you will ask for help when (not if) you need it. Ultimately, you are responsible for your learning, but knowing when and who to ask for help is part of taking hold of that responsibility. Set yourself up for success by recording your professors' office hours and contact information in your calendar or PDA or writing those hours in the space below and keeping them handy for a time when you might need help.

Reflection 8.2: Office Hours

Controlling the Technology Beast

As a 21st century student, you are immersed in the digital age. The language of technology has redefined communication, putting instant access at your finger tips— every hour of every day. Most colleges will use e-mail and text messages to keep you informed and send emergency alerts. If your school has assigned you a campus e-mail address, be sure you check it daily for important updates regarding your classes, campus life, or other issues.

While making sure you stay connected through your campus e-mail is important, your greater challenge is likely to be in disconnecting yourself from the constant chatter coming through your phone, computer, and other electronic media.   Your friends and family can easily become your constant companions, going with you to a study session in the library, to dinner with your new roommates, and to the critical lectures in your classes. Turning the noise "off" requires more than minimizing a screen, putting your phone on "vibrate," and not checking Facebook during class; it requires setting clear limits to avoid a non-stop social networking party.

As advanced as technology has become, it has not altered the fundamental characteristic of brain function that dictates that distractions are distracting. As you chat with your friends about tonight's concert during the second half of your chemistry lecture, you are not only being disrespectful to your professor, you are assaulting your brain's ability to effectively process the information that is being delivered. By keeping the electronic noise out of the classroom and out of your study sessions, you will increase the effectiveness of those learning opportunities and may actually reduce the total study time that is required.

Beyond time management, there are other reasons to think carefully about how you utilize social networking sites and programs. Remember that if your friends and family can read all about you online, future employers and officials in your college may enjoy the same privilege. Be sure that the public discussion of your life includes only those things you would be happy to chat about in a job or campus award interview.   The legacy of indiscretion in your freshman year may live on in cyberspace for years to come, creating unfortunate footnotes on your otherwise stellar record.

Access May Not Be Free

As technology brings connecting to new heights, the ethical challenges that it presents grow as well. The most common technological ethics challenge that most students face lies in the temptation of easy access to music and videos. The lure of free ownership of your favorite song and an entire season of the show everyone is watching can turn even the most ethical students into cyber pirates. While it may seem that "everyone is doing it" and that no one is hurt when you download a song illegally or when you preview a movie prior to its release in theaters, in reality, those pirating actions are the 21st century version of slipping a CD in your pocket and walking out of a store, or sneaking into a movie theater without buying a ticket.

Beyond the ethical implications, there are legal concerns as well. Your college is likely to frown on pirating behavior, and that frown may be expressed in punishments from fines to community service to expulsion. While the odds of getting caught are slim, they are not nonexistent, and government authorities are increasingly targeting college campuses to find and prosecute virtual pirates. A pirating fine is likely to far exceed the cost of honestly acquiring your entertainment in the first place. The best defense against pirating charges is to not pirate. You will protect yourself from the unwanted costs of prosecution and develop good habits of ethical conduct that will serve you well throughout college and life.

Making Resources Work for You

Your college campus offers a web of resources, which forms a collegiate community that is equipped to attend to your daily needs. From food and lodging to health, financial, and academic supports, the myriad of resources on your campus are designed to support your successful navigation of the college journey. While most of the services that are available to you were at least identified during orientation, it is easy to forget those supports later, when challenges come and confusion, frustration, or futility sets in. While you may resolve your difficulties without drawing on your campus resources, you may be more successful in resolving those difficulties if you seek the qualified supports that are available. It is not uncommon for students to graduate, look back, and wish they had taken advantage of the amazing services their institutions offered.

Take note of the facilities, personnel, organizations, and programs that might enrich your life. Some resources fill a vital need (cafeteria, medical/health center, school security), some offer recreational options (athletic facilities, performance halls), some provide financial services (financial aid office, ATM), and still others enhance your academic experience (registrar, academic advisor, library). Seek out information about each of the following resources. Meet people in person, check out facilities first hand, and take time to explore which program offerings might be just right for you. Don't wait until graduation to discover these strong threads in the fabric of your college community.

Investigating Resources and Activities

Use the next few pages as a guide to find your way around the inner workings of your school. Mark each as you visit or speak to representatives about each office, facility or service.

- ☐ Athletic Facilities: Many of the sports facilities on campus are open to students with valid ID. These might include basketball, volleyball, tennis, racquetball, and handball courts; swimming pools; weight rooms; indoor and outdoor tracks; and more. Investigate what your schools offers, the hours and other restrictions or requirements of use and get into the habit of staying active.

- ☐ ATM—For the convenience of students, ATM locations may be found on campus. Remember that unless the ATM is a part of your particular banking institution, you may be paying extra fees to check balances and withdraw money, but in a pinch, a campus ATM can be a life saver!

- ☐ Cafeteria—Food preparation and clean up is done for you if you are participating in the room and board program offered by your school. Commuters can access the same services by paying for individual meals or can sometimes enroll in a smaller meal plan than campus residents. Today's meal plans often extend beyond the traditional cafeteria to include on campus cafes, coffee shops, and bistros. Some colleges and universities have agreements with local restaurants. Find out where the food is and enjoy!

- ☐ Chapels—Most schools have a chapel where services are offered each week and special religious celebrations can be hosted. Your chapel may also offer counseling or personal support services.

- Computer Lab—Beyond the computer access provided by virtually every college and university library, various academic departments may house smaller labs, equipped with the software and hardware needs of the various majors within the department. These labs may have limited access or be available 24 hours. Check out your campus labs.

- Counseling Center—Counseling centers provide a variety of services for students who are adapting to the pressure and newness of college life, but those same services are available throughout your enrollment. Should unforeseen difficulties arise or stress become overwhelming, seek help. Assistance is often free and always confidential. Don't let a bump in the road get you off track; ask for a helping hand from your counseling center or office.

- Library—A beehive of activity, the campus library offers you physical and electronic resources to get the job of research and learning done. With electronic catalogues, most libraries allow you to begin your research before you walk through the door. While traditional books are still a vital research tool, online databases offer a wealth of relevant and cutting edge information. Attend a library orientation and find out what your library can do for you.

- Medical/health Center—Your campus medical center will offer care for many minor health needs, and in an emergency, can summon the help you need. Find out the level of care provided by your center. In addition, your health center can offer guidance and support for addressing chemical abuse and addiction.

- Parking Facilities—If you have a car on campus, you will need to know the parking rules. A $75.00 parking permit can save you daily parking violations of $35 or more. Know where and when you can park and keep a valid permit displayed at all times.

- Performance Halls—Looking for a concert, play, or interesting speaker? Check out the schedule for your on campus performance halls. Many performance majors may perform throughout the year and other talented groups and individuals may be brought to the campus by your student government or other student organizations. Attend often, and go early to get your tickets. Enjoy living in the middle of a talented community!

□ Printing—You may arrive on campus with a great printer, but if you are like many students, the first ink cartridge may be your last. Most campuses have services to print student documents. Be sure you know what printing services are offered, how to access those services, the hours of service, and the lead time required for completion of your project.

□ School Security—School security protects you and the campus. Security personnel can help you with parking and other traffic rules. After hours needs may be best addressed by your campus security officers. To ensure student safety after dark, some security offices will, upon request, safely escort students between campus buildings.

□ Student Union/Center—Student centers are generally a favorite gathering place and the venue for various activities of interest to students. Food, games rooms, televisions, small stages, and scheduled performers or speakers are often available to students at no charge. Throughout the year, student clubs and organizations may sponsor many activities in the campus student center. Watch for notices of coming events.

□ Offices and personnel—Your academic advisor, financial aid office, job placement office, office of the registrar, and academic support services are among the critical support resources you may need to access throughout college. By being aware of the breadth of services that are available, you improve your chances of finding the help you need before you need it.

□ Academic Advisor—Academic advisors can assist you in selecting a major, choosing classes, planning a career, and meeting expectations of the academic community. Meet your academic advisor early and stay connected throughout your college career.

□ Financial Aid Office—Here you will find the help you need if you are researching, applying for, and receiving scholarships, grants, or loans.

□ Job Placement—Whether you are looking for part-time work on campus as an undergraduate student, or researching your potential interview opportunities as a graduating senior, this office will be very valuable in helping you find work.

☐ Registrar: The office of the registrar manages all the aspects of your academic records: grades, transcripts, changing majors, transferring credits, and adding or withdrawing from classes.

☐ Academic Support Services: Many schools offer services to support your career as a student. These services may include private tutors, study skills classes, or skills centers. Find out what you campus offers and take advantage of any that you might need. You may find these services through the counseling center or the department of your major. Special services are often available to student athletes who face balancing a defined athletic commitment on top of a full time class schedule.

Organizations

From student government to living groups, intramural sports, campus media, and a broad array of special interest groups, your campus offers many opportunities for involvement in student life and practical experience in event planning, problem solving, team building, and other real world skills. Opportunities for involvement may include many activities that have never before been available to you. Your freshman year is a great time to stick your toe into new areas of interest or to focus your attention on long-held interests. In doing so, you will become a vital member of your college community and become engaged in activities and relationships that bring unique depth to your college experience.

One cautionary note: Approved campus groups will have to meet standards of safety and structure that may not apply to outside groups. Before getting involved in student activities that are not approved by the college itself, be sure that you verify the credentials of the organization and ensure the safety of the activity in which you will be involved. While it is not a common problem, students occasionally wander into situations that involve inappropriate or unsafe behaviors or activities. While you're expanding your horizons, be sure that you are keeping your borders secure.

Performing and Competing in College

If years of dedication, hard-work and discipline have led to the opportunity for you to compete or perform at a collegiate level, you may soon find that what you thought would be the crowning achievement of your best efforts is really a platform for renewed effort, new expectations, and continued growth. While the transition  to college is a season of change for all students, student-athletes and others participating in performance-based activities, may find it to be particularly challenging. Those who are awarded scholarships must quickly understand and respond to the reality that a scholarship represents more than funding for education, it also presents an opportunity for high level training and performance, a commitment to honor your obligations to your team, and an expectation of your best efforts. Meeting the demands of your activity participation and your academic coursework may require that you adjust your targets, improve your time management, and become an expert at utilizing your support systems.

If you hold a fine arts or other activity-based scholarship, be sure you are very clear about the requirements for maintaining that scholarship and the supports that are available to you. Requirements may vary from school to school and program to program, but it is safe to assume that you will be required to meet a minimum standard of academic performance.

If you are an athlete, the rules of your school, your sport, and the NCAA or the NAIA will dictate the standards of academic eligibility that you must meet. Your athletic

department and coaches will strive to ensure that you understand those requirements and help you meet them, but ultimately, just like other students, you are responsible for your learning. Finding ways to manage the complex demands of a student-athlete will require intentional effort, and you are wise to make use of the tutoring and other support resources made available through your athletic department.

The demands of activities are best compared to those of a full-time job and will require that you be more organized, more efficient, and more disciplined than most other students. You may have to sacrifice impromptu social events or gatherings to study, complete a research paper, or get a head start on course readings. If your friends and roommates support your disciplined efforts, consider that a bonus, and be sure that you extend that same support to others. If support is lacking, take steps to build a support system that will help you succeed.

While your roommate may navigate the road to success through trial and error, the demands of your scheduled practices, team events, and competition do not leave you much room for error and make figuring it out as you go an unlikely path to success. Your athletic activities will drive your schedule and will be largely beyond your control - demanding that you intentionally manage your class, study, sleep, and recreational time around required competition and training schedules. Like any good juggler, staying focused on your tasks and making adaptations for unexpected events will help you keep all of the balls in the air.

Professors and instructors are an essential part of your support team. Their investment in your academic success keeps you on the road to college completion. On the first day of class, you are likely to receive a course syllabus and learn about course expectations. While that may be enough information for most students, for you, the essential next step is a personal introduction to your instructor. By introducing yourself and explaining the special circumstances created by your athletic participation, you begin a critical dialogue.

Your athletic department may provide you with a form to distribute to your instructors, giving you a ready tool for initiating a conversation. If you do not have such a form, be sure that you are prepared to let your instructors know that you are an athlete, and when you are going to be absent from class for athletic competitions. Find out how you should handle missed days – do you need to turn work in early, can you turn it in late, are there times you can make-up a session through some other means? Most of your instructors will be accustomed to working with athletes and will have a system that they apply to make things work for you and for their class structure. However, occasionally you may find that an instructor is unwilling to accommodate your scheduling needs. In those cases, you may need to change your course schedule and should contact your coach or athletic academic advisor immediately for assistance.

Stay in close contact with your instructors throughout the term. Your persistent effort of communicate and give your best efforts will help your instructors to know that you are committed to success in the classroom.

There was a time not so long ago when some did not take seriously the "student" part of your student-athlete role. Today, students-athletes must be serious students and serious athletes – keeping up with both full-time "jobs" at the same time. It is a significant, but worthy challenge. By wisely managing your workload—committing your best efforts to your academic coursework and your athletic performance—you will enrich your college experience and better equip yourself for success beyond college.

Connecting for College Success

A transition is defined as a passage from one state or form to another. The last months of your life have been full of those passages – high school graduation, summer work or activities, entering college, leaving home, living with others – a tidal wave of transitions combine to create your emerging college experience. As you make those transitions, there is one critical passage that must be added to the list: adapting to your new environment by applying new learning and personal skills.

If stepping onto your college campus was like landing in a new world, that adaptation may be big. Things like moving from a small community to a big city; from a metropolis to a small town; from a community with very little ethnic diversity to a highly diverse college campus; and from a familiar family situation to a campus culture full of unique individuals with interests, passions, abilities, and concerns that may or may not align with your way of thinking, working, and being, combine to create a time of swirling change.

Successfully transitioning will require that you learn to appreciate the differences in others, be tolerant of things that are not in keeping with your ways, and be intentional about your efforts to adjust to college living and learning. College provides you with an opportunity to embrace the best of the things you have learned thus far in your life, and expand your world as you adapt to living with the environmental, cultural, and personal differences around you.

The skills you have learned in this workbook will serve you well in that process, if you use them. One of the hallmarks of college level learning is applying what you learn. When you learn things in one setting and apply them in another, you demonstrate a growing maturity in your learning. Think of this workbook as a reference tool – something you keep handy to remind you how to more successfully apply the learning skills that will lead to your college success. In addition to the content in the workbook, you have learned that making use of campus supports is vital in your college journey. From academic to personal support services, campus resources are created in response to the reality that students just like you are more successful when they have access to those resources. Making use of them does not make you weak, it makes you wise.

If you look back to your first day of high school, it may not seem that long ago. Looking forward, your journey through college will speed by as well. At the end of that road will be new transitions - passages to new places in your life, including new opportunities, challenges, and responsibilities. Those passages will be shaped in great measure by your college efforts and experiences. As you begin college, embrace the opportunities that it provides for you to grow beyond your own expectations and build a pathway to a great future. You are off to a great start; have a great year!

My Campus Resources

Athletic Facilities (weight rooms, courts, tracks, pools and other campus facilities.)

Facility:_____ Days and hours:_____

Phone:_____ E-mail address:_____

Facility:_____ Days and hours:_____

Phone:_____ E-mail address:_____

Facility:_____ Days and hours:_____

Phone:_____ E-mail address:_____

ATMs (Automatic Teller Machines)

Campus location:_____

Institution:_____ Fees:_____

Campus location:_____

Institution:_____ Fees:_____

Cafeteria, Cafes, and Other Campus Food Services

Name:_____ Location:_____

Days and hours:_____

Name:_____ Location:_____

Days and hours:_____

Name:_____ Location:_____

Days and hours:_____

Chapels

Contact name:_____ Phone:_____

Services/hours:_____

Computer Lab(s)

Location:_____ Hours:_____

Phone:_____ E-mail:_____

Location:_____ Hours:_____

Phone:_____ E-mail:_____

Counseling Center

Location:_____

Contact name: _____ Hours:_____

Phone:_____ E-mail:_____

Library(ies)

Facility:_____ Days and hours:_____

Phone:_____ E-mail address:_____

Facility:_____ Days and hours:_____

Phone:_____ E-mail address:_____

Facility:_____ Days and hours:_____

Phone:_____ E-mail address:_____

Medical/health Center

Location:_____

Contact name: _____ Hours:_____

Phone:_____ E-mail:_____

Parking Facilities

See Campus Security

Performance Halls

Name:_____ Location:_____

Phone:_____ E-mail address:_____

Name:_____ Location:_____

Phone:_____ E-mail address:_____

Name:_____ Location:_____

Phone:_____ E-mail address:_____

Printing

Name:_____ Location:_____

Phone:_____ E-mail address:_____

Cost of Printing:_____

Campus Security

Location:_____

Contact name: _____ Hours:_____

Phone:_____ E-mail:_____

Information:_____

_____

Student Union/center

Facility:_____ Days and hours:_____

Phone:_____ E-mail address:_____

Regularly scheduled events:_____

_____

Offices and Personnel

Academic Advisor

Name:_____ Hours:_____

Phone:_____ E-mail address:_____

Financial Aid Advisor

Name:_____ Hours:_____

Phone:_____ E-mail address:_____

Job Placement

Hours:_____ Services:_____

_____

Phone:_____ E-mail address:_____

Academic Support Services

Describe the services your school offers and key contact information below:

_____

_____

_____

_____

_____